The critics said—

"Displays a fine understanding of Gogol's conflict, and [Lavrin] describes the events so vividly that his book, aside from its value as literary criticism, is a moving document of human frailness and grandeur."

—*The New York Times Book Review*

"Sums up earlier hypotheses which have been advanced to account for the vagaries in Gogol's career and provides a useful introduction to the novels, stories and plays themselves."

—*The (London) Times Literary Supplement*

Janko Lavrin, a Slovene by birth, was brought up mainly in Austria and Tsarist Russia, where he commenced his career as a journalist. Settling in England after 1918, he worked on the staff of the *New Age.* He later became a member of the staff of Nottingham University College and eventually a Professor of Slavonic Languages.

His many books include studies of Dostoevsky, Tolstoy and many others.

JANKO LAVRIN

NIKOLAI GOGOL

1809–1852

COLLIER BOOKS
NEW YORK, N.Y.

This Collier Books edition is published
by arrangement with The Macmillan Company

Collier Books is a division of The Crowell-
Collier Publishing Company

First Collier Books Edition 1962

Acknowledgments

A CONSIDERABLE AMOUNT of the material dealt with in this book has been used in some of my previous essays and articles on Gogol, notably in the one which appeared in *The Republic of Letters* series (Routledge, 1925), in my Introduction to the Gogol volume in *Russian Literature Library* (Lindsay Drummond) and in my Preface to *Tales from Gogol* (Sylvan Press). Quotations from *Dead Souls, Viy, The Portrait, A Madman's Diary* and *The Marriage* are taken from *The Works of Gogol*, translated by Constance Garnett, 6 vols. (Chatto and Windus). So are some of those from *The Evenings on a Farm near Dikanka*. For the quotations from *The Sorochintsy Fair, The Nose* and *The Coach* I am indebted to *Tales from Gogol*, translated by Rose Portnova (Sylvan Press); for those from *Mirgorod*, to *Taras Bulba and other Stories* (Everyman's); and for those from *The Revizor*, to *The Government Inspector*, translated by D. J. Campbell (Sylvan Press). To the translators and publishers of these works my acknowledgements and thanks are due. Extracts from *Selected Passages*, from all the letters written by or to Gogol, as well as from the Reminiscences by various authors, have been translated by myself.

THE UNIVERSITY, NOTTINGHAM.   J. L.

Contents

Nikolai Gogol

Chapter 1

Pushkin and Gogol

1

No ONE interested in modern Russian literature can afford to ignore either Pushkin or Gogol. The very entrance of its imposing (if somewhat labyrinthine) structure is dominated by these two figures—like two great symbols of what one finds within. It was Vissarion Belinsky, the leading Russian critic of the thirties and forties of the last century, who stressed the fact that in Pushkin and Gogol Russian literature has passed 'through the most difficult and most brilliant process of its development; although it may not have reached in them its full manhood, it had left behind its adolescence and that youthful period which verges on adolescence.' Yet in spite of such a partnership, it is difficult to imagine a greater contrast than that between Pushkin and Gogol. Apart from their artistic genius, these two men seem to have little or nothing in common. On the other hand they are mutually complementary even in their differences. So much so that only by taking them together can we obtain a reliable approach to the Russian literature of the last hundred and twenty or hundred and thirty years.

Outside Russia this literature is often associated with gloomy introspection, with probings into man's psychological and spiritual underworld, where chaos, lack of balance and even madness are taken almost for granted. But an attitude of this kind is oblivious of the fact that Russia has produced in Pushkin one of the most balanced geniuses in modern world-literature; a poet who is a classic not by choice nor by conscious self-discipline (as was largely the case with Goethe), but by his very nature. He imbues everything he touches with harmony and great simplicity because, being a poet by God's Grace, he cannot help it. Chronologically he may belong to the epoch into which he was born; artistically, he is of all time. The very serenity radiated by a genius such as his is an affirmation of life in spite of all. It expresses that innate *amor fati* of his which was beyond pessimism and optimism. And no matter how painful and tragic some of his personal experiences may have been, he always knew how to transform them—through the alchemy of his aesthetic temperament—into things of beauty as detached and perfect as they could be. Yet had the Pushkin element prevailed to the exclusion of others, Russian literature would probably have assumed a simpler, more 'Apollonian' and purely aesthetic character than is actually to its credit. So, for better or for worse, a corrective was introduced by Gogol the master of prose. And since his personality represents the opposite (one is inclined to say, the necessary opposite) of Pushkin the poet, the difference between the two is bound to be reflected in their art as well. The Pushkin-Gogol contrast has indeed been responsible for a certain 'dialectical' tension in the whole of modern Russian literature, that of Soviet Russia included.

Some ten years younger than Pushkin, Gogol brought into Russian *belles-lettres,* for all his humour and laughter, those features of a brooding, tortuous and tortured mind which were foreign to the great poet. Pushkin accepted life even when displeased or disgusted with its individual aspects. He was rooted in the world around and knew how to enjoy it with a good conscience. Gogol, on the other hand, never felt quite at home either with life at large or with the world he was born into. In this respect he remained an inhibited, rootless romantic to the end of his days, and his art throve above all on the diffidence with which he regarded life and the world as a whole. Whereas Pushkin's creative impulse was one of sympathy, that of Gogol was too often prompted by hatred. Profoundly aware of the negative side of life, Pushkin preferred to depict reality from the angle of its poetic beauty, but without blinkers. Gogol, however, was in his own element only when ridiculing the world he knew; when indulging in moral pessimism and in disgust with life. Always divinely obvious, Pushkin shows in his writings a perfect sense of measure and proportion. In contrast to him,

Gogol revels in distorting the usual proportions of things by a grotesque exaggeration of certain features at the expense of others. He seems determined to impose thereby upon his readers a vision of life inseparable from his own personal attitude and struggle—the struggle with himself, with the reality around, and finally even with his own art. For such a struggle was one of the inner springs, perhaps the main inner spring, of his works. This is why he once referred to his writings as 'the history of my soul.' The differences between Pushkin and Gogol can even be extended to their social *milieux,* a brief survey of which may prove helpful.

2

Born (in 1799) in Moscow into an old and well-connected family, Pushkin was from the outset able to take himself socially for granted. He was brought up in the exclusive boarding-school at Tsarskoye Selo, and while still a youngster became thoroughly familiar with the gay life of the *jeunesse dorée* in the Russian capital. There were no pleasures his expansive nature would have denied either to himself or to others, and all his experiences—mental, emotional, sensuous, gay or sad—were distilled sooner or later into the magic draft of his poetry. Nor did he meet any obstacles on his path to literary fame. Even before he had graduated, he was accepted as an equal by Karamzin, Zhukovsky and other representatives of that gentry-literature which was to reach its crowning glory in his own works. The years between 1820 and about 1828 are doubtless the 'golden age' of Russian poetry, with Pushkin as the apex. But this gentry-period of culture was shaken to its foundations by the *débâcle* of the Decembrist revolt in 1825, after which it was gradually replaced by what is known as the intelligentsia-culture, with the voice of educated 'commoners' steadily increasing and not seldom decisive.

It would, of course, be unfair to ignore that social-economic factor which fostered such a change even apart from any revolts —the encroachment of industrial capitalism upon Russia's old patriarchal economy based on serfdom. As a result, many smaller estates were soon landed in a crisis, and their owners had to look for suitable employment elsewhere: either by joining the ranks of the bureaucracy, or by taking part in the new commercial and financial ventures even when these were (as it often happened) of an unsavoury kind. A number of impoverished noblemen became social *déclassés* or, like Turgenev's Rudin, joined the 'superfluous man' variety of the new intellectuals so conspicuous in Russian fiction in the second half of the nineteenth century.

Although only a decade divided the age of Pushkin from that of Gogol, the background against which Gogol worked was already that of the emerging intelligentsia. Born and brought up in the distant Ukraine, where the financial crisis of the small estates (that of his own parents included) was perhaps even more in evidence than in other provinces of European Russia, he could not but express his helpless wonder at a process he hardly understood. Thus in 1832, while spending a few weeks in his native district, he wrote to one of his friends: 'What a gorgeous and abundant summer. Everywhere there is a profusion of corn, of fruits and vegetables, yet people are poor and the estates are in decay, with arrears unpaid.' The height of Gogol's creative output coincided not only with this crisis but also with the mental fermentation which accompanied the advent of the intelligentsia under the leadership of that spirited 'commoner,' the critic Belinsky. It was in the circles at the Moscow University in particular that several 'commoners' and noblemen joined hands in order to counteract, as far as possible, the 'leaden regime' instituted by Nicholas I and his bureaucratic stooges. The poet Ogaryov, Granovsky, Bakunin, Belinsky—all of them one-time members either of the Stankevich or of the Herzen circle—were not slow in adopting some of the most liberal and radical ideas smuggled in from the west.[1] Even the notorious Third Section, whose task was to spy on the 'dangerous thoughts' of the citizens, proved of little avail. As if animated by the lingering spirit of the Decembrists, these radical young men braved, or at least tried to circumvent, the power of the police and of the censorship. For the very reason that a free press was impossible in Russia, a number of problems, currents and ideas which in Western Europe were vented through journalism and pamphleteering had to be incorporated by Russian authors in fiction. It did not take long before a kind of 'Aesop's language' was evolved; a language subtle enough to elude the attention of the censors but not that of the more alert readers. Even in its early stage, modern Russian fiction thus tended to go beyond mere escapism and commercialized amusement, often even beyond 'mere art.' It was Belinsky in particular who insisted (after his romantic Schelling-period) that, in addition to being true to life, literature should also serve life in its vital constructive aspects, while yet remaining literature in the best sense of this word.

We all know the 'utilitarian' temptation lurking in such an approach, but the principal Russian authors, or at least some of them, succeeded in coping with it. Instead of turning art and literature into didactic philosophy, they stated their ideas, as well as their problems (whether social, religious, moral or political), in terms of art. No wonder that before long the Russian reader began to expect from his authors, almost as a matter of course, some inner guidance or even message, not superimposed upon art but as it were organically blended with it. In taking such a course, Russian fiction certainly did endeavour to go beyond a too detached aesthetic attitude, and to become a vital force capable of influencing or even transforming man's consciousness, and through it life itself. It was Gogol who said that Pushkin was 'given to the world as an example of what a poet can be as a poet, without any other admixture; a poet not affected by the influences or conditions of some specified period, not even by his own personal character as a man, but as something independent of all that.' Yet it was Gogol also who made the statement: 'It is no longer possible to serve art, no matter how beautiful such a service may be, without understanding why and for what purpose art has been given us. It is impossible to repeat Pushkin.'

3

Having decided to serve art in this curiously present-day sense, Gogol created a current diverging from that of Pushkin, from whom he himself differed not only in his basic attitude towards life but also in his taste, his style, and even his laughter —especially in his laughter. Whereas Pushkin could laugh with a sparklingly serene gaiety, Gogol's laughter (at least after his first stories) vibrated with hidden rancour and satire. In this respect he was much nearer to Swift than, say, to Dickens, whom he so often resembles on the surface. Nor does Gogol's language show any of Pushkin's discipline and reserve. On the contrary, Gogol would not have been Gogol had he not indulged in outbursts of emotion, in gorgeous splashes of colour and in all sorts of extremes. No understatements or half-statements for him! What is beautiful is not just beautiful; it must be superbly so. The same applies, in even greater measure, to what is drab, vulgar and ugly. Whatever he may be describing, he does it, moreover, with an abandon full of nervous cadences, purple patches and piled up adjectives—like a man intent on forgetting himself in the rhythmical and melodious flow of his own words. His favourite area—especially in his early works— is along that line where prose verges on ornate rhetoric and poetry, without ceasing to be prose in its own right. It remains this side of such a hybrid as 'poetic prose.'

The pattern and texture of Gogol's ornate language have thus little in common with the simple classical manner (verging on baldness) one finds in Pushkin's narratives. For all that Gogol is one of the great masters of the word. It was he of all authors who achieved the most ingenious instrumentation of the Russian language. In Pushkin it is always the *mot juste* that determines the quality of his condensed and pregnant style, whether in verse or in prose. In Gogol, however, one is usually carried away by his orchestrated verbal wealth, no matter whether the prevailing element be 'realistic,' satirical, or ornately solemn. It would be wrong, though, to suppose that his peculiar style was due to an excess of literary culture. Unlike Pushkin, Gogol was hardly familiar with even the major figures in the European Republic of Letters. So he had to depend largely on his own artistic resources, by virtue of which he himself became one of those major figures. His very freshness may have been stimulated by the fact that he was not overburdened with the numerous aesthetic trends and theories then prevalent in Europe. But since his introspective genius was not adequately fed by mental nourishment from outside, it 'burned itself out' (to use Valery Bryusov's phrase) more quickly than he or anyone could have expected.

Last but not least, Gogol and Pushkin differed also in their grasp of the vital social and political problems of the day. For one thing, Gogol was much too self-centered and endowed, moreover, with too archaic a mind, to be able to grasp what was going on in the outside world with which he had so little in common. Pushkin, on the other hand, was not only alive to the historical currents and undercurrents of his time, but remained sufficiently detached to see them in their right perspective, no matter whether his sharp eye was turned to the events in Russia or in Europe. This does not mean that Gogol was blind to the broader issues of his epoch. Far from it. The trouble with him was that he interpreted them mainly from the angle of his own personal needs and inhibitions. And when these needs had become rather pressing, he often tried to alleviate them by preaching to others the very things he himself lacked and craved for. The blend of the artist and the preacher in Gogol was thus conditioned by certain flaws in his own nature, and their implications began to work soon enough.

4

It goes without saying that the striking 'dialectical' contrast between Pushkin and Gogol did not exclude the possibility of literary comradeship between the two geniuses. Such comradeship did exist, although it had neither the depth nor the duration of the one that is associated, say, with Goethe and Schiller.

To begin with, Gogol seems to have been strangely drawn towards Pushkin by the law of contrasts. It was not only Pushkin as his opposite, though, but Pushkin as the ideal of what a Russian might become, under favourable circumstances, 'two hundred years hence,' that appealed to Gogol's imagination. And while extolling the great poet as the promise of the highest possibilities latent in his own race, as an 'extraordinary and maybe unique phenomenon of the Russian spirit,' Gogol admired in him most of all the features he himself lacked: admired them not with envy in disguise, but with sincere and glowing enthusiasm. He needed Pushkin as a creative complement, and he knew it. This was why in 1837 Gogol complained that Pushkin's premature death had taken away 'one half of everything that might be of interest to me.' To one of his friends (Professor M. Pogodin)[2] he described his own indebtedness to the great poet as follows: 'I never undertook anything, I never wrote anything without his advice. I am indebted to him for all that is best in me.' Another of Gogol's friends, the author Sergei T. Aksakov,[3] even made (in his *History of my Acquaintance with Gogol*) the sweeping remark that the death of Pushkin was one of the main causes of Gogol's subsequent physical and mental breakdown. 'I will add,' he says, 'that in my opinion he never entirely recovered from it.' One need by no means agree with Aksakov when he insists on this having been the 'only source of the spiritual morbidity which entangled Gogol in those insoluble problems to which his great talent, exhausted by a struggle reminiscent of a hermit's, could find no satisfactory answer.' Still, there is no denying that Gogol's split-up personality must have found in Pushkin the kind of help and encouragement no one else was ever able to give him. It is also a well-known fact that Gogol even received from his poet-friend the themes for his two masterpieces, *The Revizor* and *Dead Souls*.

Pushkin's attitude towards Gogol, on the other hand, is more difficult to assess. No matter how much he appreciated Gogol's literary exploits, he found it difficult to be on perfectly friendly terms with the 'sly Ukrainian,' as he called him—hardly without reasons of his own. He also seems to have had some actual misunderstandings with him in 1836, when launching his quarterly, *The Contemporary* (*Sovremennik*), with Gogol as one of its principal contributors. Pushkin must have felt puzzled by the latter's inhibited mind, so full of repressions, hidden self-torment and the deliberate mystifications which came out in most of his dealings—whether with friend or foe. Yet Gogol's searching complexity became as important an ingredient of modern Russian literature as was the lucid naturalness and simplicity of Pushkin. The two of them together anticipated, and in a way conditioned, the general character of that literature, as well as its original contribution to the world. Gogol is the more complex of the two. So an enquiry into his mind and work is particularly worth while. In order to do this convincingly, it is best to begin at the beginning.

Chapter 2

The Vagaries of Growth

1

THE CHILD is father to the man. This dictum retains much of its truth when applied to such a character as Nikolai Gogol. Puzzling though he is, he may perhaps become less so if seen against the background and the circumstances in which he was brought up. First of all, he was not a Great Russian but a Ukrainian. His parents, who belonged to the petty landed gentry (struggling with chronic financial difficulties), lived near Poltava, in the very heart of the Ukraine. Their village, Vasilievka, was embedded in a fertile, sunny landscape where the passage of time must have seemed rather slow and life itself as remote from the hectic modern age as were the primitive inhabitants of that part of southern Russia. The whole of the Ukraine can be defined as a transition between north and south—with the stress on the latter. It is not only the climate but also the peculiar historical patina, with its flavour of the Cossack past, that makes the Ukrainians different from the Great Russians, although linguistically they are near enough to understand each other. One should not forget either that until 1654 the Ukrainians were under Polish suzerainty, which made the impact of the West stronger upon them than upon the Russians. In a way they represent an interesting amalgam of the east and southwest. Less stolid than their Great Russian neighbours, they display the carefree, nonchalant temperament of the south, as well as a strong sense of fun and humour of their own. Their artistic, especially their histrionic, gifts (in the lighter comical vein) are proverbial. They also have retained a fair amount of nomadic restlessness and spirit of adventure, probably bequeathed to them by those Cossacks who, centuries ago, used to roam the Ukrainian steppes, disputing them with the Poles, the Turks and the Tartars.

Gogol's Ukraine in particular is hardly to be thought of apart from its Cossack lore and tradition, the flavour of which once seemed to permeate her very air. The word Cossack (mentioned for the first time in the Russian chronicles of the fifteenth century) is probably of Turki origin, and it roughly meant all that is implied by the word 'adventurer.' The early bands of Cossacks did their best to corroborate such a meaning. They were a medley of fugitive peasants, outlaws and born fighters, whose exploits in the supposed defence of the Orthodox Faith often amounted to nothing more than plundering along the neighbouring Black Sea coast and even the shores of Asia Minor. Gogol's own ancestors were of Cossack stock. Their second name, Yanovsky (which he later dropped), suggests Polish affiliations too. His paternal grandfather had served as a kind of secretary to a Cossack regiment, and some of Gogol's Ukrainian motifs may have been derived from the old man's tales and yarns. In addition, two of his ancestors, Vasily Tansky and Ivan Kosiarovsky, even had some poetic products—the one in Ukrainian and the other in Russian—to their credit.

As for Gogol's parents, they could by no means boast of either excessive material or mental riches. As ready money was not always available to smaller landowners, his father had to work for a while in the Post Office. Later he seems to have occupied the position of factotum among the hangers-on of a distant relative, Troshchinsky, a retired potentate of Catherine's vintage who lived in style on a huge estate nearby. The background of Gogol's mother, too, was one of petty gentry and petty officials. She married at the abnormally early age of fourteen, because—to quote her own words—the Queen of Heaven had appeared in a dream to her future husband and had pointed her out to him. She cannot have been much more than fifteen when Nikolai was born, and a provincial girl of fifteen she remained to the end of her days: credulous, superstitiously pious, and inclined to see God's hand in everything that happened to her and hers. Many years later she confessed in her autobiographic sketch that at the time of her marriage she was quite fond of her husband; so fond indeed that she could not decide whom she liked best—him or her favourite old aunty. The spelling in her letters is often that of a semi-educated or even of a semi-literate person. It is also known that she was not always able to draw a line between her wishful thinking and the truth, especially in the things that concerned her first-born. The mental level of her husband was decidedly higher. A dreamer by nature, he had a flair for poetry and revealed some other talents as well, all of which were frustrated by ill-health and penury. When in the right mood, he would amuse his guests by telling them, very vividly, humorous stories. He also wrote—in Ukrainian—two comedies for private performance (at Troshchinsky's mansion), in which he himself acted with success. One of these comedies has appeared in print. His attempts to write plays in Russian were less convincing. Like most artistic and semi-artistic natures, he was a bad manager of his own affairs. He died in 1825.

2

It stands to reason that the offspring of such a couple could not brim over with vitality and health. Born on 20th March 1809 at Sorochintsy, Nikolai was a frail and nervous child, with a rather sickly face and pus oozing from his ears. But this made his mother pamper him all the more. She actually turned him into her fetish, and thought no end of his talents and future distinctions. As the child was on his way to boyhood she showered on him not only her maternal caresses but also her own peculiar ideas, prejudices, superstitions and archaic notions of life. In a letter he wrote to his mother in 1834, that is, at the age of twenty-four, Gogol evidently held her responsible even for the egotistic trend alluded to by him. 'I looked upon everything as if it had been created for the special purpose of gratifying me. I loved no one in particular except you, and I loved you only because nature herself had instilled this feeling into me.' After which there follow his remarks upon the religious views he owed to her: 'Once—I remember it as vividly as if it had happened a moment ago—I asked you to tell me something about the Last Judgement, and you told me most touchingly all about the blessings the virtuous would partake of. You also described in such a striking and horrifying manner the eternal torments of sinners that all my sentiments were stirred and well-nigh shattered—a fact which later on aroused in me the loftiest thoughts.'

Whatever the nature of those 'loftiest thoughts,' the undertone of Gogol's religious and would-be religious feelings remained to the end one of fear—fear of death and of hell. He himself stressed, in a letter he wrote as a man of thirty-three, that from his twelfth year on he had been treading the same path without changing in essentials, or even without doubting the things he had believed in at an early age. But whereas such archaic fears worked havoc with his imagination, he (like his mother) derived great solace from the idea that divine Providence was keeping an eye on him and all his doings. On the whole, his mind was superstitious rather than mystical or religious in a deeper sense. But for quite a number of years his notion of such a watchful protection from on high served him in good stead. Even at the 'Grammar School of Higher Learning' in Nezhin, which Gogol entered at the age of twelve, his illusion that Providence had some special plans and designs as to his future only grew stronger. It cannot be said that during the seven years of his stay there he acquired any knowledge worth speaking of, although he developed a taste for literature and excelled in the school theatricals, as an actor of comic or of decrepit old characters. At times he was given female parts to play,[4] which he did as well as he could. Yet he does not seem to have been popular with his comrades. Thin and small of stature, with a long nose on his birdlike face, he often indulged in pranks of an eccentric kind. Otherwise he was so self-conscious, secretive, and also tactless, that his schoolmates nicknamed him 'the mysterious dwarf.' But they feared his sarcastic tongue.

It was not pride, but rather his clumsiness and shyness (combined with a feeling of inferiority), that made him so 'mysterious.' For this very reason he not only found a compensation in dreams about his future greatness, but seized the first opportunity to pose as a guide and teacher even to his mother and his two younger sisters, once his father was dead. The letters he wrote them from Nezhin do not make pleasant reading. At the same time he found ways and means of asserting himself against his fellow beings too—at least indirectly—by concentrating his sharp eye on all that was clumsy and ridiculous in them. Like someone who is afraid of being laughed at by others and therefore forestalls the unpleasant situation by laughing at them, Gogol the boy soon became a past master at mimicking and making fun of grown-ups. It is here that we must look for the source of that capacity which as a writer he developed to the pitch of genius—the capacity to seize on any human trait that could be caricatured or turned into a parody.

One should not assume, however, that, for all his flirtations with Providence, he remained blind to his own faults, weaknesses and contradictions. Brooding and introspective as he was, he could not but see them even when they were least flattering to his vanity. And so from the height of dreamy self-exaltation he was prone to plunge into the depths of moral hypochondria, to exaggerate his own 'nastiness,' and to grow more and more baffled by his self-contradictory nature (of which he was yet secretly proud, since it made him so *different* from others). 'Truly I am considered a puzzle by all, and no one has unravelled me as yet completely,' he wrote to his mother in December 1827, while still at Nezhin. 'In one place I am regarded as the quietest, most unassuming and politest of fellows, while in another I may be sullen, brooding and awkward, and in yet a third a chatterbox and a regular nuisance. Think of me as you like; it is only my true life-work that will reveal my true character.' The problem of such life-work rose before him early enough. Yet strange though it may sound, his ambitions then had little to do with a literary career. As if overwhelmed by the pomp and magnificence of Troshchinsky, he thought that civil service in Petersburg was the only emporium where he could assert his own value and show the world who and what he was. With this in view he made the requisite arrangements and hoped for the best.

'I do not know whether my plans will come true,' he wrote in 1827 to his friend Vysotsky, who was already in the Tsarist capital; 'whether I too shall live in that heavenly spot, or whether the wheel of fortune will cruelly fling me, together with the self-contented mob—what an awful thought—into the realm of nobodies, thus confining me to the dark quarter of obscurity.' In the same over-dressed style he wrote to his maternal uncle Kosiarovsky: 'Cold sweat pours down my face at the thought that I shall perhaps perish in the dust, without making my name known by a single remarkable deed; to live in this world without making my existence worth while would be too terrible for words. . . . I have meditated on all sorts of careers and offices of State, and have decided to take up jurisprudence. As I see it, the latter would offer me more opportunities for work than any other profession, and here alone could I become a benefactor to humanity.'

What exactly he meant by 'benefactor to humanity' is difficult to gauge. He himself was in the dark about it. Still, a year later, in the autumn of 1828, Gogol left for Petersburg, thus turning a new page in his life.

3

The change was indeed staggering, but hardly in the sense he had expected. The 'heavenly spot' of his day-dreams soon proved to be more like a hell for an ungainly-looking young provincial without money and without connexions. Far from being welcomed as a prospective Troshchinsky, he was unable to obtain even the post of a humble clerk. Instead of living in a palace on the Neva embankment, he had to put up with a drab fifth-floor dwelling. Like so many *déclassés* of the impoverished gentry class, he knew he had to fend for himself, yet he only kept piling one disappointment upon another. In despair he tried his luck as an actor, but for various reasons failed to pass the test. So he had to part with his hope of a theatrical career as well.

It was in the midst of such trials and tribulations that he embarked upon a literary venture simply because he had already exhausted all other possibilities. As it happened, he had brought from Nezhin an immature narrative poem written under German influence and even with a German title, *Hanz* (sic!) *Kuechelgarten*. Bearing traces of Voss's *Luise*, the poem describes the fate of the young Hans, who goes out into the world and after a number of adventures returns disillusioned to his idyllic native village, marries his sweetheart Luisa and is presumably happy ever after. The theme, with its triumph of the patriarchal idyllic principle, is not unlike Gogol's own dilemma. On leaving the Ukraine he was landed in a cold and callous Petersburg whence he looked back with nostalgia to the pastoral land of his youth; but, in contrast to his hero, he was unable to return, since such a step would mean giving up all his dreams of a career. As the poem was devoid of originality or even talent, no publisher was brave enough to take it. So Gogol printed it at his own expense (under the *nom de plume* of Alov). Hoping to conquer fame with one stroke, he even had the impudence to write a laudatory *Publisher's Preface*, which he concluded with the remark: 'We are proud to offer to the world a chance to acquaint itself with this product of a young talent.' But the world would not take the chance. Only two newspapers (one in Petersburg and the other in Moscow) condescended to mention the booklet, and this in such merciless terms that Gogol hurried to collect all the copies he had distributed among the bookshops, and burnt them forthwith.

Even more unaccountable was his next escapade. As though resentful at the blow inflicted upon his literary ambition, Gogol seemed to have thought—in the summer of 1829—of expatriating himself altogether and even of writing in a foreign tongue. 'If my work is ever printed, it will be in a foreign language,' he wrote to his mother, when asking her to send him some details about Ukrainian life. The idea of fleeing abroad proved too attractive to be resisted. Having no funds of his own, he embezzled a sum of 1,450 roubles his mother had sent him for payment to the Custody Board, and sailed to Lübeck, which he reached on 1st August 1829. He may have planned a longer journey, as far perhaps as America, but he contented himself with going to Hamburg instead. The money kept melting away, though, and after some three months in Germany Gogol sailed back to Petersburg. However strange this adventure, the excuses he sent to his mother were stranger still in their naïve blend of lies and cunning. He tried to make her believe that he suffered from a dangerous chest-complaint which he hoped to cure abroad. The mighty will of God was drawn into the embezzlement almost as a matter of course. Yet in another letter written only a few days earlier Gogol, without even a mention of his chest, switched the limelight on to a *femme fatale* whom he was impelled to follow wherever she went. The sickeningly pompous tone of the letter needs as little comment as the tale with which he hoped to placate his mother. 'To you alone I can tell it. You know that I am endowed with a firmness of will which is rare in a young man. . . . Who, then, could have expected such weakness on my part! But I saw her. . . . To look at her only once—such was my sole desire; and my desire grew amidst painful restlessness the poison of which I cannot describe. . . . I saw that I had to flee from my own self in order to keep alive and preserve at least the shadow of peace in my devastated soul. With reverence I recognized the Invisible Hand coming to my aid, and I blessed the path which was thus pointed out to me from on high.' And so on, and so forth. This guidance from on high was reinforced by a bit of snobbery, since the lady responsible for it all had to be of highly aristocratic birth. 'No, I will not tell you her name. She is much too exalted for anyone, not only for me.'

This cheap melodramatic bluff, with 'fits of madness,' 'awful inner torment,' and the 'craving to get intoxicated by a single glance of hers,' was concocted by Gogol in a manner which was likely to appeal to his mother's provincial tastes. Yet his journey bore no fruits of any kind. It only proved to be another frustration, and an expensive one at that. But once back in

Petersburg, Gogol had to keep the wolf from the door. The same trials started again, and this time not without success. In November 1829 he obtained the post of minor clerk in the Ministry of Internal Affairs at a salary which was much too small to cover even his most pressing needs, such as buying a warm overcoat in order to brave the severity of the Russian winter. In April of the following year he was shifted to another department, but without any substantial increase in salary. He is even supposed to have been associated for a while with the Third Section—the bugbear of all liberal-minded intellectuals. It is true that the incrimination to this effect came from the notorious time-server and *canaille journaliste*, Faddei Bulgarin,[5] as late as 1854—two years after Gogol's death. On the other hand, Gogol's character was 'elastic' enough for him to commit any sort of *faux pas*, not so much from wickedness as from irresponsibility—the same kind of irresponsibility which had made him embezzle his mother's money just in order to gratify his sudden urge to travel. Yet, amidst his new efforts to arrange his life in a tolerable manner, something unforeseen took place: Gogol stumbled as it were upon his latent genius and upon the only vocation he was really fit for.

4

What happened was that he once more tried his luck in literature—not in poetry, but in prose. As folkloristic motifs were then in fashion, he began writing tales of Ukrainian life strongly flavoured with 'local colour.' He gathered details about it with the zest of a collector, and quite a number of these were supplied by his own mother. His first tale, *St. John's Eve*, appeared at the beginning of 1830 in *The Fatherland's Annals*, and was subsequently included (with some alterations) in the first volume of his stories. In 1831 he was introduced by the poet Delvig (in whose *Literary Gazette* he wrote) to Pushkin's friend, Professor Pletnyov.[6] He also became acquainted with the lady-in-waiting, Alexandra Osipovna Rosset, whose interest in *literati* often made her render such services in mitigating the stupidity of the Russian censors that she was nicknamed *Notre Dame aux bons secours de la littérature russe en détresse*. At Mademoiselle Rosset's, Gogol met both Pushkin and Zhukovsky. Pletnyov secured for him, in 1831, the post of junior history-master at the Patriotic Institute, a school for girls of noble families. But he was so badly paid that he had to make ends meet by private tuition.

Count V. A. Sollogub, himself an author,[7] tells us in his reminiscences how he first met Gogol in 1831. The budding celebrity was engaged at the time as tutor to a half-witted son of Sollogub's aunt at Pavlovsk near Petersburg. And this is what the encounter was like: 'We entered the nursery where at the writing-desk the tutor sat. He was showing his pupil pictures of various animals, imitating at the same time their bleating, bellowing, grunting, etc. "This, my darling, is a ram; do you follow? A ram—*bah, bah*. . . . This here is a cow, you know; a cow—*moo, moo, moo* . . ." And the tutor went on imitating the animals' sounds with a peculiar and rather queer gusto. I confess the scene filled me with sadness, at the pitiable lot of a man who was compelled to do this sort of work in order to earn his daily bread. I quickly left the room, hardly paying any attention to the voice of my aunt, who introduced the teacher to me by his full name: Nikolai Vasilyevich Gogol.'

So, in spite of his contact with the literary world, Gogol's existence still remained unsettled. But uncertainty, penury and despondency only helped him to conjure up tales and impressions of the Ukraine of his childhood, with all its mirth, fun and laughter, as the only escape from the reality he had to endure. Such was the origin of his stories, *Evenings on a Farm near Dikanka*, the first volume of which appeared in 1831 and the second in the following year. This time Gogol really woke up one morning to find himself famous, or at least on the road to fame.

Chapter 3

The First Triumph

1

GOGOL HIMSELF must have been surprised at the immediate success of his book, but there were quite a few reasons to account for it. The temperamental vivacity of his style was one of them. The other was the 'native' colour and flavour of his stories, which could not but appeal to those readers in particular who were anxious to welcome any signs of Russian narratives independent of Western examples. For until as late as the twenties of the last century the influence of Western European literature was paramount. And even when Russian fiction began to emancipate itself, the process did not seem an easy one. Marlinsky,[8] for example, took his themes from Russian life, but he still indulged in the rhetoric and heroics of the imported 'furious' school. Further attempts at freeing the Russian short story were made by Odoevsky, Polevoy, Pogodin, Dahl and Pavlov, most of whose products were put into the shade by even the first collection of Gogol's tales.

The appearance of these coincided, moreover, with a growing taste for Ukrainian themes, especially of a picturesque and romantic kind. The tales in *Evenings*, with their peculiar medley of lyrical, farcical, folkloristic and would-be folkloristic elements, provided an answer to such a demand, even though their comicality was still rather primitive: the comicality of people who are fond of horseplay and of funny situations for their own sake. On the other hand, Gogol put into these first writings of his all the verve of a born story-teller and impersonator in one. And while at work he must have raked up the impressions of his boyhood, the Cossack tales and yarns, the demonology of the peasants, as well as of the Ukrainian farces current in his native province. Further elements were probably gleaned by him from the comic Ukrainian travesty of Virgil's *Æneid* by Ivan Kotlyarevsky;[9] from Orest Somov's fantastic tales about devils and demons; and above all from the Ukrainian puppet-theatre or *vertep*, which was still popular in the days of Gogol's youth. The *vertep* was actually a Ukrainian equivalent of the Polish *szopka* (the 'stable') and consisted of a portable wooden box divided into an upper and a lower floor. Its function was to give nativity plays, manipulated by theological students, who at Christmas time carried the boxes from village to village and performed a number of comic interludes as well. Whereas the upper floor of the *vertep* was reserved for the nativity play itself, the floor below was for farcical intermezzi. These were at times surprisingly 'realistic' in their topical allusions and local colour, their stock characters being the devil (of the folk-imagination), the swaggering Pole, the ubiquitous comic Jew, and of course the reckless Cossack. Also the comic names of Gogol's heroes, verging at times on the obscene (Sverbiguz, Golopupenko, etc) are redolent of popular farces.

It was out of such and similar elements that Gogol wove the fanciful pattern of his tales, in which the world of peasants and Cossacks mingles in a grotesquely amusing whirl with the realm of devils, witches, ghosts and goblins, most of them taken straight from the folk-tradition. Furthermore, some of these stories are not 'written'—they are 'told.' Gogol uses as the supposed author a village bee-keeper, the 'redhaired Panko,' whose tone, inflections, turns of phrases and even humorous facial expressions are duly rendered at times. But this manner, which normally would lead to the colloquial *skaz* (a yarn stylized in the language of a peasant or a lower middle-class person), is not sustained to the end. Sooner or later it passes into the literary language proper, interspersed with Gogol's own outbursts of lyrical moods and descriptions. At least one of the stories is modelled also on the pattern of an enlarged folk-ballad, as it were. Hence the frequent change in the style and texture of his early prose. Yet Gogol's narrative vein is so strong as to bridge all contrasts of this kind and to subdue the readers to his own artistic laws and caprices.

We may no longer share the excessive enthusiasm of Gogol's first readers. But, all things told, we can well understand why the two volumes of *Evenings* were hailed as something unusual even by men of letters. The critic Belinsky, for example, did not mind comparing the charm of these tales with the effect left on one by Shakespeare's *Midsummer Night's Dream*. Pushkin himself, whose caution equalled his discrimination, gave them unstinted praise. 'Here we have real and not forced gaiety, without anything artificial or stiff,' he wrote apropos of *Evenings*. 'And how much poetry and sensitiveness there is in some of the passages! All this is so new in our literature that I have not yet got over my surprise. I congratulate the readers on a truly delightful book.'

2

In each volume of *Evenings* there are four narratives: *The Sorochintsy Fair, St. John's Eve, A May Night* and *The Lost Letter* in the first; *Christmas Eve, A Horrid Vengeance, Ivan Fyodorovich Shponka and his Aunty* and *A Bewitched Spot* in the second. The feature common to most of them is Gogol's mixture of the fantastic with the observed and the 'real.' Yet instead of inventing his themes or motifs, he—for the most part—only made dexterous use of the material collected from various outside sources, in many cases from his own mother. Speaking generally, his imagination was not so much of the *inventive* as of the *intensifying* kind—to the extent of making him magnify his ideas and impressions into something like spooks, by which he himself was often haunted. Years later (at the age of forty) Gogol referred in his correspondence to this trait of his by saying: 'I see, for example, that someone has stumbled; my imagination immediately gets hold of the fact, begins to develop it into most horrid apparitions, which torture me, deprive me of my sleep and waste my strength.' Gogol always found it more difficult to invent than to 'collect,' observe and intensify, which did not in the least impair his creative verve or vision. He made this clear when stating (in *An Author's*

Confession): 'I never invented by mere imagination. Only in those things was I successful which I took from reality and which I based on the data I knew. I could fathom a man only when I had seen the minutest features of his exterior. Still, I never *painted* a portrait by simply copying it. I *created* portraits, but I did so on the basis of consideration rather than on that of imagination. The more details I had seen and considered, the better were my productions. My mind is in this respect thoroughly Russian; that is, prone to derive rather than invent.' It matters little where and in what quantities he had collected ingredients for his *Evenings*. The important thing is that he knew how to organize them into a spirited interplay of romantic, 'realistic,' lyrical, comic and also gruesomely haunting elements.

What these haunting elements were like can be gathered from the story *A Horrid Vengeance*, and to some extent from *St. John's Eve* (slightly reminiscent of Tieck's *Liebeszauber*). Yet all this is offset by the delightful gaiety of his other tales. Take the buffoonery of *The Sorochintsy Fair;* the fantastic helter-skelter of village lads, drunken worthies, Cossacks, devils and witches in *The Christmas Eve;* or such racy yarns as *A Bewitched Spot* and *The Lost Letter*. But when Gogol himself steps in, the texture of the narrative changes, and his exuberant lyricism verges, now and then, on rhetorical *clichés*. The very first story, *The Sorochintsy Fair*, opens with a description of a Ukrainian summer-day in precisely this style. 'How languidly hot are the hours when at noon the day sparkles in silence and sultriness, and the blue and infinite ocean of sky, bent over the earth like a voluptuous dome, seems to have fallen asleep in tenderness, clasping the beautiful earth in an airy embrace!' etc, etc. But even passages of such spurious nature-lyricism are redeemed by the rich, melodious and rhythmical quality of Gogol's prose. So one does not mind if his pictures have, as a rule, little to do with real nature. His landscapes, including his famous descriptions of the Dnieper and of the Ukrainian May night (invariable items in all Russian Anthologies), are largely operatic. At times they have the magic of landscapes seen in dreams. Yet even when they pretend to be realistic their emotional tonality is highly subjective. Hence the profusion of hyperbolism and of purple patches which, but for Gogol's verbal music, would make one think of 'technicolor.' All the same they, too, point to the subjective character of Gogol's first book.

3

Gogol himself said of his *Evenings* that the 'cause of the gaiety in my first writings is to be sought in my own inner need. I became a prey to fits of melancholy which were beyond my comprehension. . . . In order to get rid of them I imagined the most comic things: funny characters in the funniest situations one could think of.' The second feature, which he does not mention yet which is prominent in the book, can be defined as his nearness to the collective Unconscious and to the archaic pattern of thought. This is why some of his stories are told on the plane of folk-tales, with all the marks of folk-mythology and of symbols reminiscent of primitive archaic dreams. Such a propensity was not devoid of certain dangers—dangers which played havoc with Gogol's mind at a later stage. For the time being, however, it accounted much more for that freshness of his which could not but impress his more cultured and more sophisticated colleagues. The demons, witches and wizards parading in his tales are taken for the most part straight from the people. The Devil in particular, though treated farcically, had for Gogol the same undeniable reality as for a Ukrainian peasant. So had those heavenly powers which Gogol obviously regarded as stronger than the evil spirits walking here on earth and intent on doing mischief. In *A May Night*, for instance, a peasant lad comforts his sweetheart with the remark that 'God has a ladder reaching from heaven right down to earth. The holy archangels put it up before Easter Sunday, and as soon as God steps on the first rung of it, all the evil spirits fall headlong and sink in heaps down to hell. And this is how it is that at Christ's festival there isn't one evil spirit on earth.' This kind of infantile and at the same time poetic mythology, believed in by the Ukrainian masses, seems to have appealed to Gogol's mind. What is more, the symbol of the ladder retained so specific a meaning for him that he used it in his private letters and referred to it even on his death-bed. It is at this juncture that traces of folk-poetry in Gogol's early stories should also be mentioned: of the Ukrainian *dumy* (lyrical folk-ballads) as well as of the Great-Russian *byliny*.

Gogol's archaic frame of mind, deeply related to the primitive collective Unconscious, emerges with particular emphasis in *A Horrid Vengeance*—one of the creepiest stories ever written. Here the obsession with crime and incest comes out in symbols reminiscent of folk-tales and folk-ballads. It actually ends with a would-be ballad, sung by a blind beggar in order to convey the meaning of the happenings narrated. As in *St. John's Eve*, here too the intrusion of evil, indelible in man and in life, looms up with the nightmarish power which leaves little room for the comic even as a relief. Such a relief is plentiful, however, in his other stories. One of these, *Ivan Shponka and his Aunty*, deserves a mention on account of its subject-matter, and also because it anticipates all the features of the so-called realism, typical of Gogol's later and greater works. The background of the story is one of the Ukrainian landed gentry Gogol knew from his own home, while the hero is a shy and undersexed ex-officer whom his aunty induces to woo a neighbour's daughter. As the wooer is not quite sure of being able to do justice to the matrimonial duties expected of him, the very words 'marriage' and 'wife' are enough to throw him into a cold perspiration. Yet woo he must. His fears overwhelm him at last in a nightmare where his prospective wife, like a Proteus, assumes all sorts of shapes and forms, cropping up again and again in the most unexpected places—just to remind him that an escape is impossible.

First, he dreamed that everything was whirling with a noise around him, and he was running and running, as fast as his legs would carry him. . . . Now he was at his last gasp. . . . All at once some one caught him by his ear. 'Aie! who is it!' 'It's I, your wife!' a voice resounded loudly in his ear—and he woke up. Then he imagined that he was married, that everything in their little house was so peculiar, so strange: a double-bed stood in his room instead of a single one; his wife was sitting on a chair. He felt queer: he did not know how to approach her, and then he noticed that she had the face of a goose. He happened to turn aside and saw another wife, also with the face of a goose. Turning in another direction he saw yet a third wife; and behind him was still another. Then he was seized by panic; he dashed away into the garden: but there it was hot; he took off his hat, and—saw a wife sitting in his hat. Drops of sweat came out on his face. He put his hand in his pocket for his handkerchief, and in his pocket too there was a wife; he took some cotton-wool out of his ear—and there too sat a wife. . . . Then he suddenly began hopping on one leg, and Aunty, looking at him, said with a dignified air: 'Yes, you must hop on one leg now, for you are a married man.' He went towards her, but his aunt was no longer an aunt but a belfry, and he felt that someone was dragging him by the rope on the belfry. 'Who is pulling me?' Ivan Fyodorovich asked plaintively. 'It's I, your wife. I am pulling you because you are a bell.' 'No, I am not a bell,' said the colonel of the P. infantry-regiment, who happened to be passing. Then he dreamed that his wife was not a human being at all but a sort of woollen material; that he went into a shop in Mogilyov: 'What sort of stuff would you like?' asked the shopkeeper. 'You had better take a wife that is the most fashionable material! It wears well. Everyone is having coats made of it now.' The shopkeeper measured and cut off his wife. Ivan Fyodorovich Shponka put her under his arm and went off to a Jewish tailor. 'No,' said the Jew, 'that is poor material! No one has coats made of that now. . . .' Ivan Fyodorovich woke up in terror, not knowing where he was; he was dripping with cold perspiration.

One could write a whole treatise on Gogol's attitude towards dreams and its coincidence with the various aspects of modern psycho-analysis,[10] but this would take us beyond the scope of the present book. A few words should be said, however, about the consequences this first literary success had on the author's character (or lack of character).

4

Gogol could not but feel gratified by the tangible proof that fate had not after all relegated him to the 'dark quarter of obscurity.' Yet success came too suddenly to have a good effect upon him. As if anxious to make up for his former doubts and mishaps, he now assumed (wherever it was safe) the manner of a fop, or even of a *nouveau riche* from the provinces, with shockingly bad manners and a pretentious style in dress. In the letters he wrote to some of the well-known authors at the time his own fame was in its initial stage (1831–32), one comes across passages which are unpleasantly insinuating. In an otherwise vivid letter to the poet Zhukovsky, who was tutor to the Tsarevich and therefore stayed with the imperial family at Tsarskoye Selo, he regretted the obstacles preventing their meeting and said, with Asiatic obsequiousness, what he would do if he were able to pay a visit to him. 'Oh, with what enthusiasm I would then wipe the dust off your shoes with the hair of my head, would lie down at the feet of your Excellency and catch with my greedy ear the sweet nectar [of poetry, pouring] from your mouth.' No wonder that even so good-natured and tolerant a person as Sergei Aksakov, who met him for the first time in 1832, was unable to form a good opinion of Gogol the man, however much he may have admired him as a writer.

'The external appearance of Gogol was not in his favour at the time,' he says. 'A crest of hair on his head, carefully clipped kiss-curls on his temples, clean-shaven lips and chin and an enormous, over-starched collar gave an artificial expression to his face; there seemed to be something made-up and cunning in him. In his costume, pretensions to dandyism were noticeable. I remember his bright, motley waistcoat with its big watch-chain. On the whole, something in him made me refrain from that warmth and expansion in which I often indulge. At his request I took him to see Zagoskin.[11] On our way there Gogol surprised me by his complaints about all sorts of diseases from which he thought he suffered—even past recovery. As he seemed to be in perfect health, I looked at him with wondering and incredulous eyes. "What is wrong with you?" I asked. His answer was that his ailments were caused by his intestines.'

Nor was Aksakov's son Constantine (the famous Slavophil) impressed by Gogol. He found the young celebrity rude and overbearing when talking to ordinary mortals. This was, of course, only one facet of Gogol's nature. For it did not take long before he was in danger of falling into the opposite extreme—into doubts and vacillations which made him underestimate himself and the value of his own work. All he could do was to counteract moods of this kind by new literary ventures. These he took up without delay and with such a work-fever that the period between 1833 and the end of 1836 comprised the most creative years of his life. Apart from the writings he finished during that time, he made plans for the works he intended to complete in the future, plans which included at least the beginning of his great novel *Dead Souls*. He also made use of the social opportunities which only a few months earlier had been beyond his wildest dreams. The circle he moved in at St Petersburg consisted of such leading figures in Russian culture as Pushkin, Zhukovsky, Prince Vyazemsky, Baron Delvig and Professor Pletnyov, all of whom appreciated Gogol's talent even when they were less sure of his character. In Moscow, again, he was petted by the more conservative and patriarchal Aksakov family, the historian Professor Pogodin and their Slavophil *entourage*.

Pondering on such a change, Gogol could not but see in it another proof that God, or divine Providence, was taking special care of him and of his future. This being so, he thought of enlarging his activities by becoming a benefactor of humanity not only as a writer but also as a teacher, whose voice would resound from the platform and stir the hearts of his listeners. He actually applied in 1834 for the vacant chair of history at Kiev University, although he must have known full well that he lacked the qualifications required for such a post. For some unaccountable reason the Minister of Education, Count S. Uvarov, gave him the chair of history—not at Kiev, but at the University of St Petersburg.

5

It all looked like a huge joke. But Gogol, now being personally involved, refused to see the comic side of it. It is true that his opening lecture—on the Middle Ages—was delivered with a rhetorical aplomb which kept the audience spell-bound. But the expectations aroused by it were far from justified, and the students were not slow in drawing the necessary conclusions— by no means flattering to the 'professor.' As a matter of fact, the only history in which Gogol felt more or less at home was that of the Ukrainian Cossacks, and even here his approach was more romantic than scientific. Nor had he enough energy to fill the gaps in his knowledge by stubborn toil. Greeks and Romans meant little or nothing to him. And as for the deeper springs of history, he clung to his faith in the workings of Providence, buttressed by a sentimental and puerile hero-worship. Anyway, after the success of his first lecture the interest of listeners began to flag, until his incompetence was evident even to the blind. Gogol's position became awkward, as we can see from the testimony of no less a person than the great novelist Turgenev, who happened to be one of his students. Observant as he was, Ivan Turgenev left an amusing account of that professorship, or whatever we might call it.

'In 1835,' he says, 'I was one of Gogol's students at the University of St Petersburg. To tell the truth, his lecturing was rather queer. First of all, out of three lectures Gogol invariably missed two; and even when he was present in the lecturing hall he did not speak, but only muttered incoherently about something, while showing us little steel engravings of Palestine and other eastern countries. He was all the time in a terrible confusion. We were convinced (and justly so) that he knew nothing about history and that our Professor Gogol-Yanovsky was an entirely different person from Gogol the writer—already famous on account of his *Evenings on a Farm near Dikanka*. During our final examinations he sat with a handkerchief round his head and simulated toothache. There was an expression of extreme pain on his face, and he never opened his mouth. Professor T. P. Shulgin examined his students instead. I can still see, as if it were happening now, Gogol's thin figure, his long nose, and the two ends of the handkerchief surging above his head in the shape of two ears. He must have understood the awkwardness of his own position, for he retired in the same year. Yet this did not prevent him from exclaiming: "Unappreciated I took the Chair, and unappreciated I leave it." '

There can be no doubt that the elements of bluff were inherent in Gogol's character and kept reappearing in various disguises at various stages of his life. His 'professorship,' whatever its ulterior motives, was one of them. Fortunately for him and for literature, it did not last long. Relieved of it, he was able to concentrate on literary activities. The more so because, meanwhile, his reputation had been enhanced by his second collection of narratives under the title of *Mirgorod* (1835).

Chapter 4

Mirgorod

1

LIKE *Evenings on a Farm near Dikanka*, *Mirgorod* was published in two volumes, each of them containing only two longish narratives, *The Old-World Landowners* and *Taras Bulba* being the first; *Viy* and *The Quarrel of the Two Ivans* in the second. Gogol referred to these stories as a continuation of *Evenings*. And so they are after a fashion, only this time with Mirgorod (a little town in his native district) as their centre. They also show some new aspects of Gogol's art, and above all a somewhat clearer division between the romantic and the 'realistic' side of his work. *The Old-World Landowners*, for example, looks to all intents and purposes like a genre picture in the style of the meticulously realistic Dutch school. Yet if we go below its surface, we are likely to detect Gogol's camouflaged romantic mood. First of all, he started writing this story in 1832—the year in which he visited his native Vasilyevka. This may explain the idyllic and patriarchal atmosphere with which he imbued the whole narrative. For instead of a plot we have here but elaborate portraiture of an old couple—a kind of Ukrainian Philemon and Baucis who may have been modelled on Gogol's own grandparents. The stress is thus laid on characters and also on the bucolic and pleasantly vegetative side of that patriarchal existence which was already beginning to look shaky in an age of encroaching capitalism.

The couple in question, Afanasy Ivanovich and Pulkheria Ivanovna, know little and care less about the outside world. They have become so much part and parcel of their idyllic farmstead, of the landscape and 'nature' around that, with all their gentility, they are hardly quite human. Even their mutual attachment, strong though it be, is a matter of habit rather than anything else. Yet they both know happiness and contentment.

43

To all appearance Gogol, disgusted by the noise and whirl of a big town, had turned these two people into an embodiment of his own idea of peace and of that unruffled pastoral world which he had known in his childhood. Hence the sympathy with which he describes the old couple and their uneventful daily existence.

I can see now the low-roofed, little house, with its verandah of slender, blackened tree-trunks surrounding it on all sides so that in case of thunder or hail the shutters could be closed without your getting wet; behind I see fragrant wild-cherry bushes, whole rows of small fruit-trees laden with purple cherries and with an ocean of dark-blue plums; I see luxuriant maples, under the shade of which rugs are spread for repose, and in front of the house the spacious yard with short fresh grass, through which paths have been trodden from the store-house to the kitchen, and from the kitchen to the living-rooms; a long-necked goose drinking water, with her young goslings soft as down; the picket-fence hung with bunches of dried pears and apples, and rugs put out to be aired; a cart full of melons standing near the store-house; the unyoked ox lazily lying beside it. All this has for me an indescribable charm, perhaps because it is far away and because anything from which we are separated is pleasing to us.

While depicting the old couple in this setting, Gogol describes even their defects—their gluttony for instance—with a good-natured amusement. The well-nigh subhuman vegetative undercurrent of the story actually comes out in their continuous craving for food. The whole of their existence, especially that of Afanasy Ivanovich, revolves round food, and their day is punctuated by innumerable meals, with few or no intervals between them.

'Well, Pulkheria Ivanovna, isn't it time perhaps for a snack of something?' Afanasy would say to his better-half almost immediately after breakfast.

'What would you like to have now, Afanasy Ivanovich? Would you like lardy cakes or poppy-seeds, or perhaps salted mushrooms?'

An hour before dinner Afanasy Ivanovich would have another snack, would empty an old-fashioned silver goblet of vodka, would eat mushrooms, various sorts of dried fish and so on. They sat down to dinner at twelve o'clock. Besides the dishes and sauceboats there stood on the table numbers of pots with closely-covered lids so that no appetizing masterpiece of old-fashioned cookery might be spoilt. At dinner the conversation turned on subjects closely related to the dinner. 'I fancy this porridge,' Afanasy Ivanovich would say, 'is a little bit burnt. Don't you think so, Pulkheria Ivanovna?' 'No, Afanasy Ivanovich; you put a little more butter to it, then it won't taste burnt; or have some of this mushroom sauce; pour that over it!' 'Perhaps,' said Afanasy Ivanovich, passing his plate; 'let us try how it may be.'

After dinner Afanasy Ivanovich went to lie down for an hour, after which Pulkheria Ivanovna would take a sliced water-melon and say: 'Taste how nice this melon is, Afanasy Ivanovich.'

'Don't be too sure of it, Pulkheria Ivanovna, because it is red in the middle,' Afanasy Ivanovich would say, taking a good slice. 'There are some that are red and are not nice.'

But the melon quickly disappeared. After that, Afanasy Ivanovich would eat a few pears and go for a walk in the garden with Pulkheria Ivanovna. On returning home, Pulkheria Ivanovna would go off to see to household affairs, while he sat under an awning turned towards the courtyard and watched the store-room continually displaying and concealing its interior and the serf-girls pushing one another as they brought in or carried out heaps of trifles of all sorts in wooden boxes, sieves, trays and other receptacles for holding fruit. A little later he would send for Pulkheria Ivanovna, or himself go to her and say: 'What shall I have to eat, Pulkheria Ivanovna?'

And so on. The passages read like an apotheosis of gluttony,[12] but with no implication of moral censure, since the whole of it is but an example of man's 'return to nature,' to the contentment of the vanishing or vanished patriarchal ways. Gogol contrives to make us thoroughly fond of the couple and to feel sorry for poor Afanasy when death bereaves him of his affectionate better-half. It does not take long, though, before he joins her in the world beyond. The final note of sadness passes into one of amused indignation when the active 'up-to-date' heir, immediately on his arrival, introduces all sorts of modern improvements—with the result that the farm soon goes to rack and ruin. Gogol's sarcasm aimed at things new was only another aspect of that nostalgia for the past which he indulged in and idealized in *Taras Bulba*.

2

But for its size *Taras Bulba*[13] might pass for a historical novel —a genre which for a long time found little favour with the classicists in Russia. Nor were its early phases either original or significant enough to claim our attention. The sentimental historical narrative, introduced by Karamzin at the end of the eighteenth century, was replaced by its declamatory-romantic counterpart (Marlinsky, Glinka, Polevoy) until, towards 1830, the influence of Sir Walter Scott stepped in: superficially in Zagoskin, Lazhechnikov and Bulgarin, but solidly in Pushkin and, as far as it went, in Gogol. Both were able to assimilate that influence creatively: Pushkin in his classics, *A Captain's Daughter* and *Dubrovsky*, and Gogol in *Taras Bulba*—perhaps the most melodious prose-work in Russian. But whatever Scott's influence upon him, Gogol went back to the old times in an escapist spirit: in order to 'beat the present' (as he put it in a letter) by the past. In his eagerness to underline the colourful Cossack past, he paid so little attention to historical truth as at times to confuse the fifteenth, sixteenth and even seventeenth centuries. On the other hand, he brought out its poetic truth, flavoured with the *souffle* of the Ukrainian folk-ballads. Gogol called his narrative an 'epic,' and with some justice. Belinsky actually went so far as to compare *Taras Bulba* with Homer. The French critic Sainte-Beuve, too, referred to it as a Cossack *Iliad*. Perhaps because its heroes show the same kind of spontaneity and pre-moral 'beyond good and evil' as those of Homer. Their passions are equally simple and elemental, but against their own Ukrainian background, as Gogol saw it, or wanted to see it. The narrative is, moreover, all of a piece. Each part adds not only to the compactness of the tale, but also to the typicality of the characters.

The principal figure Taras in particular seems to have sprung right out of heroic times, inseparable from bards and sagas. We meet him first when he welcomes his two sons Ostap and Andriy on their return from the school at Kiev—quite in the Cossack style of the sixteenth or seventeenth century. For the first thing he does is to entice the two sturdy fellows into a fight to test their strength. Pleased with the result, the restive old warrior decides there and then to take both of them to the Cossack headquarters at the Sech. And so Taras, his two sons and a small retinue of Cossacks set out at dawn, riding through the plains where 'no plough had ever passed over the unmeasurable expanse of wild growth.' Gogol spares neither words nor colour when extolling the beauty of the steppe. With the same relish he depicts Taras's arrival at the boisterous Cossack headquarters; the ruse whereby he advocates an immediate expedition against the Poles (partly in order to give his two sons a chance); the revel of the drunken Cossacks; the election of a new leader; the gruesome yet tragi-comic *pogrom;* the miraculously resilient Jew Yankel, and finally the entire Cossack Army on the move until it halts at the Polish fortress of Dubno.

During the siege of Dubno Andriy learns that the Polish *belle* who had won his heart while he was still at Kiev happens to be in the beleaguered and starving city. Without hesitation he takes as much food as he can carry and, once in the fortress, joins the Poles. During the battles that follow Ostap is captured by the enemy, while Andriy is cunningly ambushed in a wood where his own father shoots him dead. The Cossacks are beaten and dispersed. Taras is grievously wounded, but his prodigious vitality saves him. As soon as he feels well enough, he is smuggled—with Yankel's help and in the guise of a foreigner—into Warsaw, where his son Ostap is due to be executed. Yankel bribes the prison guards, but the plan to liberate Ostap is frustrated by the old Cossack's careless tongue. While watching his son's execution, Taras decides to avenge it in true Cossack fashion. He keeps his word by reappearing on the Polish border with an Army of a hundred and twenty thousand men whose hetman or leader he has become. Raging with the fury of an elemental force let loose, he plunders and ravages one district after another. But this time, too, the Cossack army is beaten. Taras himself is taken prisoner on the bank of the Dnester and tied to a tree which his captors set on fire. When he is already licked by the flames, he sees with satisfaction that his comrades have succeeded in getting into skiffs in which they hastily row away, beyond the reach of their foes.

> Broad is the river Dnester, and in it are many deep pools, dense reed-beds, clear shallows and little bays: its watery mirror gleams, filled with the melodious plaint of the swan; the proud wild goose glides swiftly over it; and snipe, red-throated ruffs, and other birds are to be found among the reeds and along the banks. The Cossacks rowed swiftly on in the narrow double-ruddered boats—rowed stoutly, carefully shunning the sand-bars, and cleaving the ranks of the birds which took wing; they rowed, and talked of their hetman.

Such is the end of this romance in which Gogol's ornate style reaches its climax. The plot is of course as melodramatic as are the themes of those ballads or sagas of which it reminds us. It is only when the melodrama descends to stock-in-trade *clichés*, as it does in the love-affair between Andriy and his Polish sweetheart, that Gogol's descriptions are less satisfactory. 'He (Andriy) raised his eyes and saw a beauty such as he had never beheld in his life, black-eyed and with a skin as white as the snow in the dawning flush of the sun.' But such was Gogol's usual weakness whenever he wanted to render the charms of a beautiful girl or woman. Matchless in his portraits of old and ugly people, he was strangely weak as a painter of normal beautiful women—a feature which remained typical of all his works, largely for personal reasons.

As far as is known, Gogol had no first-hand experience of woman's love. Undersexed as he seems to have been by his physical constitution, he did not care much for women as women. Nor did he ever rid himself of the infantile attachment to his mother, however patronizingly he may have treated her in his letters. Unable to find a normal outlet, his *libido* is supposed to have assumed the form of those auto-erotic practices which not only caused him intense moral suffering but served as a further barrier between him and women.[14] These he divided, in his romantic manner, into angels and demons, while still continuing to treat love and marriage either as a parody or as a melodrama.

In one of his early fragments, *The Woman* (1830), for instance, he answers the question, 'What is Woman?' with a shower of high-falutin' platitudes.

> She is poetry, she is thought, and we are merely her reflection in reality. Her impressions shine upon us, and the more strongly and intensely they are reflected in us, the nobler and better we become. . . . Whenever man's soul dissolves in the ethereal bosom of a woman's soul; when it finds in her its own father, the eternal God, its own brothers, feelings and phenomena which nothing on earth could express before, what happens then? Then the soul revives within itself its forgotten harmonies, its forgotten heavenly existence in the bosom of God himself, and makes it infinity.

Rhetorical drivel of this kind can be unravelled by any competent psycho-analyst. What concerns us here, though, is Gogol's inability to integrate sex and love as far as he himself was concerned. While love tended to become purely abstract and 'divine,' his sex (or rather the sexual self-abuse from which he suffered) struck him as being from the devil and therefore the more sinful the greater was its hold on his own will and imagination. The polarity of the cleavage, with its unhealthy erotic effects, could thus hardly be avoided. But for this very reason he also had glimpses into that 'demoniacal' element of woman as a symbol of sex, of evil, of hell and perdition, which he tried to embody in his ultra-romantic story *Viy*.

3

In this narrative, as in *A Horrid Vengeance*, we are again in the realm of dream-symbols and of 'private mythology' arising out of the collective Unconscious. The figure of Viy himself is such a symbol, taken from Ukrainian folklore. According to Gogol's (not quite reliable) note, Viy is a 'colossal product of folk-imagination: the chief of the gnomes whose eyelids are of such length as to touch the ground.' These have to be lifted by outsiders in order to allow the gnome to see at all; but once his eyes are open nothing is hidden from them, and whoever they behold is doomed to perish. This motif is here combined with another product of folk imagination—the witch whose enthralling beauty is in the service of evil. As narrative, *Viy* is less organic in its structure than *A Horrid Vengeance*. It also suffers from a lack of convincing motivation. On the other hand, its sinister symbolic-mythological character is relieved by Gogol's comic description of the Cossacks and particularly of the Kiev divinity students, one of whom, the stolid 'philosopher' Homa, is the hero of the tale.

While staying overnight at a lonely inn, Homa is ensnared by an old witch who contrives to fly on his back over the steppe. During the flight he manages, however, to get on *her* back and he takes revenge by beating her with all his might, until the old hag falls exhausted to the ground. Here she is suddenly transformed into a dazzling beauty, but with all the signs of having been battered almost to death. Puzzled by it all, the 'philosopher' thinks it wise to hurry back to Kiev while he is safe. But no sooner is he there than a Cossack chief in the steppe urgently summons him to come and stand in a church a three nights' vigil over his daughter. Homa recognizes in the deceased the beautiful witch he himself had beaten to death. The situation looks hardly inviting, but as no escape is possible he is ready to discharge his duty as best he can. It does not take long before all sorts of necromantic horrors set in. The climax during the first as well as the second night in the locked church is reached when the witch's corpse suddenly revives and, amidst incredible hubbub, begins to grope for the 'philosopher.' But Homa, whose intrepidity is supported by brandy, has drawn a magic circle within which he feels reasonably safe. During the first two nights, at any rate, he remained beyond her reach. The final test took place in the third night, when the corpse rose amid wild invocations and

> a countless host of monsters flew into the church, filling the whole building with a fearful noise of flapping wings and scratching claws as they circled about searching everywhere for the philosopher. He could see the form of some enormous monster covering the whole of one wall: it was enveloped in its own tangled hair, as in a wood, and through the net of hair two eyes with slightly raised brows peered out in a horrid fashion. Above him something like a huge bubble hung in the air, with a thousand claws and stings protruding from its middle. Black earth clung to them in clots. All were looking at Homa, but unable to see him, surrounded as he was by his magic circle.
>
> 'Bring the Viy!' rang out the voice of the corpse, 'go and bring the Viy in!' And suddenly all became silent in the church. A kind of wolfish howling was heard in the distance, and soon the church resounded with heavy footsteps. Casting a glance downwards, Homa saw them leading forward some burly, thick-set, bowlegged figure covered with black soil: his earthy arms and legs stuck out like powerful sinewy roots. He walked heavily along, stum-

bling at every step. His eyelids hung down to the very ground. Homa noticed in terror that his face was of iron. They led him by the arms straight to the place where Homa stood.

'Lift my eyelids! I cannot see!' said Viy in a subterranean tone, and all the throng dashed forward to raise them for him.

'There he is!' shouted Viy, and pointed with his iron finger at him. The whole crowd flung themselves upon the philosopher. Lifeless he crashed to the floor: his soul flew out of his body from sheer terror.

The story ends with the remark that after that the monsters dashed to the windows, but as the second crowing of the cocks had already passed they were too late: so they remained stuck in the doors and windows, while the church became so overgrown with wild vegetation that no one was able to reach it.

It is, perhaps, not too far-fetched to regard the Viy as the dreaded father-imago which has become aware of Gogol's secret erotic practices and may therefore crush him on the spot. Even the monsters, stuck fast in the doors and the windows, symbolize, as it were, all sorts of 'vices' the moral hypochondriac Gogol was anxious to shake off and could not. As years went on, his hypochondria only kept growing. Yet from now on he refrained from the nightmare-symbolism à la Bosch, so prominent in *Viy*.

He turned to more 'realistic' themes and methods instead, as exemplified by the story of the two quarrelling Ivans. And here, again, Gogol arranged all the details in such a manner as to make his very realism symbolic as it were of his own attitude towards life and the world.

4

The Story of the Quarrel between Ivan Ivanovich and Ivan Nikiforovich is actually an anecdote, intensified into something more significant than its title might suggest. When it first appeared in a miscellany in 1834, it was referred to by Gogol as one of the unpublished yarns of *Evenings*. He reissued it in *Mirgorod* with several alterations, while yet preserving the basic tone of a *skaz* or a 'told' story. This time Gogol obviously wanted to overcome the escapist idyllism of his previous tales by a satirical treatment of characters and of their background. Gogol's very use of hyperbolism is here no longer an expression of lyrical exultation but of ironic eulogy. The comic effect is achieved by the assumed solemnity with which he talks about the most trivial things. He laughs at people as they are, or at least as he sees them. But in his laughter one can feel the rancour of a romantic who takes revenge upon life because it has failed to come up to his expectations. The idyll of *The Old-World Landowners* is replaced by a picture of rural existence more in Hogarth's style. We are among the same petty gentry-folk, and the grotesque angle from which they are now shown only stresses the vacuum of their lives which can be, and are, thrown out of gear by the merest bagatelle.

Like several others, this story, too, was written by Gogol 'on the basis of consideration rather than on that of imagination.' Gogol, who always took his goods where he found them, was partly indebted to *Two Ivans, or the Passion of Litigation* (1825) by another Ukrainian writing in Russian, Vasily T. Narezhny. He may even have personally known the characters he described. According to one of his commentators (Kulish), there actually lived in Mirgorod two worthies who started a long lawsuit because one of them had been called 'goose' by the other. The two litigants went on with the process mainly because they enjoyed their neighbours' repeated efforts to reconcile them. They often drove to the lawcourt quite amicably in one and the same carriage. Gogol, however, ignored all this and construed his story in such a manner as to vent through it his own subjective view and vision of human existence. The very relish with which he describes the features of his characters is full of amused contempt. The two Ivans are exact opposites in their looks and habits, but in essence they both represent two burlesque specimens of the same human zoo.

Ivan Ivanovich is tall and thin; Ivan Nikiforovich is rather shorter in stature but makes up for it in thickness. Ivan Ivanovich's head is like a radish, tail down; Ivan Nikiforovich's like a radish with the tail up. Ivan Ivanovich lolls on the balcony in his shirtsleeves after dinner only; in the evening he dons his pelisse and goes out somewhere, either to the village shop, where he supplies flour, or into the field to catch quail. Ivan Nikiforovich lies all day in his porch; if the days are not too hot he generally turns his back to the sun and will not go anywhere. Ivan Ivanovich is a very refined man, never utters an impolite word in conversation, and is offended at once if he hears one. Ivan Nikiforovich is not always on his guard. On such occasions, Ivan Ivanovich usually rises from his seat and says, 'Enough, enough, Ivan Nikiforovich! It's better to go out at once than to utter such godless words!' Ivan Ivanovich has large, expressive eyes the colour of snuff, and a mouth shaped something like the letter V; Ivan Nikiforovich has small, yellowish eyes quite concealed between heavy brows and fat cheeks and his nose is the shape of a ripe plum. If Ivan Ivanovich treats you to snuff, he always licks the cover of his box first with his tongue, then taps on it with his finger and says as he raises it, if you are an acquaintance, 'Dare I beg you, sir, though I have not the honour of knowing your rank, name and family, to do me the favour?' But Ivan Nikiforovich puts his box straight into your hand and merely adds, 'Do me the favour.'

Gogol collects and condenses as many details as he needs in order to show the comic automatism of the characters concerned and to expose the anti-life around by means of his laughter. The two Ivans move before us like two comic puppets endowed with life, and—in spite of their different tastes and habits—their friendship is such 'as though the devil himself had tied them together with a rope.' But it all came to an end on a pettiest pretext. Ivan Ivanovich wanted to buy from his friend an old gun the latter would not part with. In the altercation that followed, Ivan Nikiforovich called his genteel and touchy bosom-pal a goose. The effect was disastrous. 'Ivan Ivanovich could no longer control himself. His lips quivered, his mouth lost its usual V-shape and became like an O; he glared so that he was terrible to look at.' To the consternation of all honest folk in Mirgorod, both of them started a lawsuit, in the course of which they accused each other of the most murderous deeds and intentions. But the *gorodnichy* (town governor) hit upon the idea of inviting the two enemies to a specially arranged gala-dinner. They came. No sooner had the dinner been finished than they both rose in order to run away and thus avoid each other's company. They would have done so had not the host already taken strategic measures to prevent it. One Ivan was pushed towards the other so discreetly that the situation began to look promising. Ivan Nikiforovich was even feeling for his snuffbox with the idea of offering it to his enemy ('Do me the favour!'). But Ivan Ivanovich would not surrender without making some edifying remarks.

'Was it not an insult,' he said without raising his eyes, 'when you, my dear sir, insulted my honour and my family with a word which it is improper to repeat here?'

'Permit me to observe in a friendly manner, Ivan Ivanovich'—here Ivan Nikiforovich touched Ivan Ivanovich's button with his finger, which clearly indicated the disposition of his mind—'that you took offence the deuce only knows at what, because I called you a goose—'

The very mention of this word spoiled everything. Ivan Ivanovich departed fuming. The guests realized that further efforts were of no avail. So litigation was resumed and dragged on and on. Many years later Gogol happened to pass through the sleepy little town and saw the two Ivans. Both of them were now decrepit old men, but they still continued their quarrel, hoping to ruin one another. It was both ridiculous and sad. The very day on which he left, Mirgorod looked sad enough to damp even his protective laughter.

The lean nags known in Mirgorod as post-horses started producing with their hoofs, which were buried in a grey mass of mud, a sound very displeasing to the ear. The rain poured in torrents upon the Jew seated on the box covered with a rug. The dampness penetrated me through and through. The dreary barrier with a sentry-box, in which an old soldier was repairing his weapons, was passed slowly. Again the same fields, in some places black where they had been dug up, in others of a greenish hue; wet daws and crows; monotonous rain; a tearful sky, without one gleam of light! . . . It is gloomy in this world, gentlemen!

Chapter 5

The Impact of Petersburg

1

'IT IS GLOOMY in this world, gentlemen,' became from now on the undertone of Gogol's attitude towards life as a whole. It determined the character of his further writings, and even that of his peculiar laughter. For in contrast to affirmative and in essence benevolently disposed humour, the ironic comicality of Gogol's brand went hand-in-hand with hidden spite, as well as with those vindictive and indicting moods which began to protrude in his Petersburg stories. Whereas the prevailing atmosphere of *Evenings* and *Mirgorod* was that of the south, the five narratives on the themes he gathered in the foggy Russian capital are written in a different key. There was only one more story, *The Coach* (written in 1835 and printed in the first issue of Pushkin's *Contemporary* in 1836), to which he gave a south-Russian setting, and with real fun at that, no matter how trifling the theme. It all starts with the arrival of a cavalry regiment in a sleepy little town. The foppish local landowner Chertokutski —himself a former cavalry officer, but cashiered as the result of an incident usually termed an 'unpleasant story'—is all astir with excitement. He introduces himself to the 'brother officers,' drinks, fraternizes and swaggers with them, and has the time of his life.

Anxious to palm off on the General a Viennese coach, he invited during one of the bouts His Excellency and a number of officers to come and have lunch the next day at his house in the district. The officers' bout lasted longer than it should and ended in the usual style: when at three o'clock in the morning the guests began to disperse, the 'drivers had to carry several persons bodily, as if they were parcels of merchandise. And Chertokutski, in spite of all his nobility, bowed so deeply sitting

57

in the carriage and with such a waving of his head that, when
he arrived home, he brought back in his moustache two buds
of burdock.' Rather late in the day he was aroused from the
sleep of the just by the news that a whole cavalcade of officers
was approaching his farm. He only now remembered his hasty
invitation. But as nothing had been prepared for the guests he
ran out of the house in his night-shirt and hid in the very coach
His Excellency intended to buy. The merry company was nonplussed on hearing that the hospitable gentleman was not at
home. Still, the Viennese coach was there to be inspected, and
so His Excellency wanted to have a look at it. Its appearance
did not tally with the glowing praise he had heard the day before, but perhaps the inside was more remarkable. The inner
part was duly uncovered, and there was the fugitive host himself, huddled up in his night-shirt and numb with embarrass-
ment.

'Ah, here you are,' said the General. He slammed the carriage
door, and off he galloped, with his cavalcade.

This anecdotal material was turned by Gogol into a gem
which shows a perfect balance between the comicality of situations and that of characters, not to mention his tone and inflec-
tion at their best. His treatment of the military atmosphere alone
is worth something. Dickens would have delighted in it. For
here Gogol's irony is devoid of that rancour which became so
conspicuous a feature of his Petersburg tales: *The Portrait, The
Nevsky Prospect, A Madman's Diary, The Nose*, and *The
Greatcoat*. The first three of these appeared in his next book,
Arabesques (1835), which—apart from the stories mentioned
—represents a motley collection of essays: on art, history,
poetry and even geography.[15] Gogol was obviously probing his
vein of a potential teacher and preacher, but hardly with many
original thoughts of his own. His views on art, for instance,
echoed the romantic theories of Schelling and Wackenroder,
both of whom had ardent adherents in Russia, notably in Moscow. His essay on Pushkin was good, though. One could have
singled out a few impressive passages in some of his other
discourses as well. Still, most of it was dilettantism, covered as

it were by a somewhat 'professorial' aplomb. 'If essays of this kind are called science, then may heaven preserve us from such science,' said Belinsky when referring to the didactic side of the book. He praised, however, the three stories, undoubtedly the best part of the miscellany. Of these, *The Portrait* should be dealt with first.

2

The paradox about *The Portrait* is that, while being the most derivative and 'Western' among Gogol's narratives, it still remains one of his most personal key-stories. It shows some traces of E. T. A. Hoffman's *Die Elixiere des Teufels*, of Maturin's one-time best-seller *Melmoth the Wanderer* (it appeared in Russian in 1833), and of a few other foreign works, including Washington Irving's tale *The Adventure of the Mysterious Picture*, the Russian translation of which (1829) bore the title *The Mysterious Portrait*. Yet whatever the ingredients or external influences, Gogol assimilated and adapted them to his own inner needs. He did this at a time when he was already perturbed by something like an incipient moral crisis, as well as by a growing awareness of the principle of evil inherent in existence itself and as if inseparable from it. Also the romantic idea of a synthesis between art and religion (or what he understood by religion) here became conspicuous as one of his personal problems. In *The Portrait*, moreover, Gogol explored, according to his lights, the relation of art not only towards his own inner life, but towards life in general. Hence the story deserves, perhaps, a closer scrutiny than its intrinsic value would make one at first suppose.

The Portrait actually includes two stories, each of them more or less complete in itself and yet explanatory of the other. As a link between them serves the mysterious usurer Petromikhali, who is the agent of the Evil One and who therefore emanates evil and ruins all who have anything to do with him.[16] It so happened that the struggling young painter Chartkov acquired the usurer's portrait. From its frame there suddenly fell a sum of money sufficient to make him achieve worldly success as a fashionable portrait-painter. Having yielded to temptation, Chartkov killed his talent and became merely a rich, self-satisfied celebrity. But he had a rude awakening. As an acknowledged judge in matters of art, he was invited one day to express his opinion concerning a picture sent in by an artist who, disregarding fame and success, lived only for his vocation. The picture proved to be so perfect that Chartkov was numb with amazement. For the first time he realized what a price his own worldly success had cost him. Contrite and humbled, he went home with the resolve to start afresh: to make up for the talent he had wasted in his chase of fame and money. But when he set to work his brush would no longer obey him. His creative power was dead, and there was no way of reviving it. Mad with regret, he soon became possessed by a helpless envy with regard to all true talents. He began buying up their pictures in order to destroy them, and heaven only knows to what lengths he would have gone had he not died in the grip of insanity. Such was the penalty he incurred for having prostituted the talent given to him from on high.

The second story which follows is but a romantic explanation of how the usurer's portrait originated and what eventually happened to it. It is told by a young man (the son of the painter who had been responsible for the picture) to a crowd of customers at an auction where the same ill-fated work of art is exhibited. He tells them all he knows about the usurer and how, one day, a painter—the narrator's own father—was suddenly called to Petromikhali's. The usurer, now on his death-bed, was anxious to have his portrait done regardless of the cost. The artist agreed. But when the eyes were finished he became so terrified by some infernal power which had passed into them that he refused to go on with his work and ran away in horror. It transpired that the portrait of the man was nothing less than the embodiment of evil, intent on perpetuating itself even after its agent was dead. The painter realized that without his knowing it his art had served the evil one, and this guilt hung over him like a nightmare. In order to redeem it he entered a monastery, took the vows and submitted to the severest asceticism. Only after he had finished a holy picture in the monastery church did the eyes of the money-lender cease to haunt him. No one ever found out what had happened to the portrait itself. Many years later, however, the artist-monk imparted the secret to his son—with many a precept reflecting Gogol's own mortal fears and inhibitions.

> 'Listen, my son. For long years the Antichrist has craved to be born. . . . He is choosing man himself for his dwelling-place, and appearing in those people whose angel seems to have abandoned them at their very birth and who are branded with the terrible hatred towards men and everything that is the work of the Creator. Such was that strange money-lender whom I, accursed that I was, dared to depict with my sinful brush. It was he, my son; it was Antichrist. . . . In those loathsome, evil eyes the devilish feeling persisted. Marvel, my son, at the terrible power of the devil. He strives to make his way into everything; into our deeds, into our thoughts, and even into the inspiration of the artist. Innumerable will be the victims of that hellish spirit that lives on earth unseen, without form. It is the same black spirit which forces itself upon us even in moments of the purest and holiest meditation. Ah, if my brush had not abandoned its hellish work he would have done us even more evil, and there is no human power to resist him; for he is choosing that time when the greatest calamities are coming upon us. Woe to poor humanity, my son!'

Then follows the silliest romantc rigmarole: the monk's prophecy that the demoniacal power of the portrait could be undone provided someone would tell all about it at the new moon in fifty years' time—neither more nor less. And since the story told by the narrator happens to coincide with exactly such an anniversary, the portrait begins to vanish from the canvas and is replaced by an insignificant landscape instead. Fortunately, Gogol wrote a less silly ending for the second rewritten version of the story, which appeared in *The Contemporary*

(1842). According to it, the narrator at the auction had hardly finished the last sentence when he

> turned his eyes to the wall in order to glance once more at the portrait. The entire throng of auditors made the same movement, seeking the strange portrait with their eyes. But to their extreme amazement, it was no longer on the wall. An indistinct murmur and exclamation ran through the crowd, and then was heard the word 'stolen.' Someone had succeeded in carrying it off, taking advantage of the fact that the attention of the spectators was distracted by the story.

The evil symbolized in that portrait was thus to continue unchecked.

The antiquated romanticism of this narrative need not blind us to some of those motives which, some ten years later, made Gogol definitely switch over from aesthetic to the moral values and even to admonitions not unlike those described above. *The Portrait*, therefore, contains a number of camouflaged personal elements which, incidentally, are not absent from the other two stories either.

3

To a superficial reader both *The Nevsky Prospect* and *A Madman's Diary* (especially the second) would appear to belong to realistic fiction. And so they do in a way, but only with the reservation that the impulse behind Gogol's 'realism' is one of romantic negation and disgust. The wounded idealist in him does not set out to describe reality in a detached, objective manner. What he is after is to discredit reality; to prove that the latter is not worthy of acceptance. Like *The Portrait*, *The Nevsky Prospect* too is one of Gogol's key-stories and bears traces of Western influences, above all of Hoffmann's *Der Goldene Topf* (*The Golden Pot*), whose hero Anselmus resembles the frustrated dreamer in Gogol's story.[17]

The narrative opens with a gorgeous description of the Nevsky thoroughfare—one of the liveliest and most enticing spots in Europe. But it is also one of the most deceptive—deceptive at all hours, and particularly when 'night falls in masses of shadows on it, throwing into relief the white and sun-coloured walls of the houses, when all the town is transformed into noise and brilliance, when myriads of carriages roll over bridges, postilions shout and jolt up and down on their horses, and when the demon himself lights the street lamps to show everything in false colours.' It is on such an evening that two friends, one an artist and the other an officer, see on the Nevsky two pretty women passing by. While the dashing lieutenant Pirogov rushes after the unknown blonde, the artist Piskaryov follows the younger girl in whom he has discovered the very perfection of beauty. He falls so deeply in love that life without her presence loses all meaning for him. So he is determined to find out who she is and where she lives. He starts his searches and finally discovers that she lives in a house of ill fame, playing the *métier* of an ordinary prostitute and bespattered with all the filth clinging to it. Unable to bear his own disappointment, and least of all such a degradation of beauty, the artist takes to drugs and finally commits suicide.

A different adventure was in store for the flippant young lieutenant Pirogov (one of Gogol's best drawn early portraits). It turned out that the blonde pursued by him was the wife of an ultra-punctilious German artisan, who always got up at seven, kissed his spouse only twice in twenty-four hours, and got drunk only on Sundays. Pirogov went on with his advances under the very nose of the blonde's husband. One Sunday, however, he was caught by the already tipsy German and his two equally drunken associates, all of whom gave him a thorough thrashing. Beside himself with anger, Pirogov set out at once to lodge a complaint with the General and to demand punishment for such an outrage committed upon an officer. But while on the way he

went into a café, ate two jam puffs, read something out of the *Northern Bee* and left the café with his wrath somewhat cooled. Then a pleasant fresh evening led him to take a few turns along the Nevsky, and by nine o'clock he had recovered his serenity and decided that he had better not disturb the General on a Sunday. And so he went to spend the evening with one of the directors of the control committee, where he met a very agreeable party of government officials and officers of his regiment. There he spent a very pleasant evening, and so distinguished himself in the mazurka that not only the ladies but even their partners were moved to admiration.

Piskaryov's drama is thus accompanied by Pirogov's farce in the spirit of romantic irony, which in Gogol's work assumed an accent of its own. A mixture of hidden tragedy and of farce now became more and more prominent in that 'laughter through tears' which is usually associated with Gogol. A foretaste of it can be found in *A Madman's Diary*, undoubtedly the best of the three stories discussed.

4

Gogol (probably inspired by Hoffmann) at first intended to write *The Diary of a Musician*. This at any rate was the early title of the story, written in 1833–34, which he then altered and issued as *A Madman's Diary*. Its hero is not a Hoffmannesque mad musician, but a poor copying-clerk—the kind of 'little man' in the office whom Gogol knew so well from personal experience. As the author's own exploits and mishaps in the bureaucratic world were of recent date, it was natural that he should have made an attempt to lampoon the higher representatives of that species; and above all to portray those office-drudges who were not even allowed to have a self, however humble, of their own. In this story Gogol tried to combine both, but with a stress on the 'little man,' whose tragedy is the more effective because it is treated in a pathetically comic vein.

The elderly copyist Poprishchin (for this is the hero's name) is one of such drudges confined to the 'realm of nobodies.' In spite of his unprepossessing appearance—his wrinkled face, clumsy manners and tufts of hair resembling hay—he secretly falls in love with his chief's daughter. He has not the remotest chance of being even noticed by the pretty girl (there are too many young men of exalted rank who snatch away all the good things in this life); but his thwarted ego finds a compensation in day-dreams, all of them revolving round his love. Gradually the world of actuality recedes in favour of his own dream-world: of the phantoms and delusions heralding his madness. Instead of facing things as they are, with all the shocks awaiting him, Poprishchin barricades himself behind his wishful thinking. By the time the betrothal of his Excellency's daughter to a *Kammer-junker* (Gentleman of the Chamber) takes place, Poprishchin's reason is already in a hopeless muddle. Having read in the papers about the Spanish troubles in 1833, he ponders with much concern about the political situation in that country, until he suddenly discovers that he himself is His Majesty Ferdinand VIII, the fugitive king of Spain, whose throne has been usurped by Don Carlos. From that moment on, his imaginary exaltation is enough to compensate him for all the blows he has to endure. Anxious to live up to his rank, he assumes the majestic demeanour of a ruler who, exiled though he is, still remains a ruler of men. Besides, he feels sure that a deputation of Spanish grandees will sooner or later come and put him back on his throne. The 'grandees' actually arrive and take him to the lunatic asylum. But here, too, he interprets everything in the light of his own royal status. During the painful cold-water cure he realizes for a moment his true position; a shriek of despair comes from his breast; he wants to escape, but it is only for a moment. Madness closes on him again, and the story ends with his idiotic exclamation: 'Do you know that the Bey of Algiers has a boil right under his nose?'

The passage of Poprishchin's muddled state of mind to one of madness is rendered by Gogol with such intuition as if he himself had passed through it. The process we watch is really a short cut on the part of an utterly frustrated human being back to infantilism by way of madness as his only outlet from an unbearable situation. Simultaneously Poprishchin's senseless gibberish hides a great deal of erotic symbolism as well—symbolism in which unconscious verbal associations play their part. The grotesque character of his entries only makes his case the more poignant, perhaps with a scarcely disguised hint at Gogol's own retarded and distorted erotics. What could be more interesting from a psycho-analytical angle than the following passage of Poprishchin's diary!

When I was alone I decided to occupy myself with affairs of State. I discovered that Spain and China were one and the same country, and it is only through ignorance that they are considered to be different kingdoms. I recommend everyone to try and write Spain on a bit of paper; it will always turn out China. But I was particularly distressed by an event which will take place tomorrow. Tomorrow at seven o'clock a strange phenomenon will occur; the earth will fall on the moon. The celebrated English chemist Wellington has written about it. I must confess that I experience a tremor in my heart when I reflect upon the extreme softness and fragility of the moon. You see the moon is, generally, made in Hamburg, and very badly made, too. I am surprised that England hasn't taken notice of it. It was made by a lame cooper, and it is evident that the fool has no idea what a moon should consist of. He put in tarred cord and one part of olive oil; and that is why there is such a fearful stench all over the world that one has to stop one's nose. And that is how it is that the moon is such a soft globe that man cannot live on it and that nothing lives there but noses. And it is for that very reason that we can't see our noses, because they all live in the moon. And when I reflected that the earth is a heavy body and when it falls it may grind our noses to powder I was so overcome by uneasiness that, putting on my shoes and stockings, I hastened to the hall of the Imperial Council to give orders to the police not to allow the earth to fall on the moon. The grandees with shaven heads whom I found in great numbers in the hall of the Imperial Council were very intelligent people, and when I said: "Gentlemen, let us save the moon, for the earth is trying to fall on it!" they all rushed to carry out my sovereign wishes, and several climbed up the walls to try and get at the moon; but at that moment the High Chancellor walked in. Seeing him they all ran in different directions. I, as King, alone remained. But to my amazement the Chancellor struck me with his stick and drove me back to my room! So great is the power of national customs in Spain!'

5

Independently of *The Arabesques*, Gogol published two more narratives, *The Nose* and *The Greatcoat*, with bureaucratic Petersburg as their background. The first of these, written between 1833 and 1836, was printed in the third issue of Pushkin's *Contemporary*,[18] and its very title connects it with the above-mentioned passage from *A Madman's Diary*. It is the most grotesque story Gogol ever wrote. Its ambiguous symbolism, puns and jokes, on the other hand, allude to inhibitions which can best be discussed in medical terms and are therefore of less concern to us. The story itself is thought to be a parody of the romantic doubles *á la* Hoffmann and probably also of Chamisso's *Peter Schlemihl*—a tale in which the shadow ran away from its owner. But apart from all this Gogol here made literary use of the pattern of a nonsensical (or seemingly nonsensical) dream. His earlier draft, which was rejected by *The Moscow Observer*, actually ended with the remark that the burlesque adventures of the nose which had run away from its owner, were only a dream. But Gogol altered much of it in 1836, and again in 1842, when the narrative came out in his collected works. Needless to say, there existed by that time a considerable 'nosological' literature, including the requisite passages in *Tristram Shandy*, which Gogol must have read in a Russian translation. It is known, moreover, that Gogol was fond of listening to smutty anecdotes, and the 'symbolic' aspect of the nose may have intrigued him precisely on account of its connexion with sex. In *Evenings* the story about the undersexed Ivan Shponka remained deliberately unfinished. So in *The Nose* Gogol resumed the motif once again, and with all the unconscious or half-conscious fear of impotence cropping up in its ambiguous dream-symbolism.

The hero of *The Nose*, Major Kovalyov (a smug military-bureaucratic upstart), belongs to a more enterprising species than Shponka. He is nearer to Pirogov in *The Nevsky Prospect* —flippantly vulgar in his attitude towards the fair sex, although not adverse to contracting a profitable marriage, as long as the emphasis rests on the word *profitable*. Yet one morning something happens which jeopardizes his ambitions in a most distressing manner.

> Collegiate assessor Kovalyov awoke comparatively early and made the sound *b-r-r-r-r* with his lips, which he always did on waking, although he himself did not know the reason for it. Kovalyov stretched himself and called to his servant to give him a mirror which was standing on the table. He wanted to look at a pimple which had suddenly appeared on his nose the night before, but, to his great amazement he saw that there was a completely smooth place instead of the nose.

Thrown out of all ordinary walks of life by such an accident, Kovalyov began his comic search for the missing appendage, but in vain. The nose, having so meanly deserted him, lived an independent existence as a great personage—a State Councillor in fact—and refused to acknowledge any acquaintanceship with the distressed Kovalyov when accosted by the latter and cautiously reminded that it should know its proper place. Kovalyov then made the conjecture that the person responsible for it all must have been a woman: the Staff-Officer's wife Podtochina who wanted him to marry her daughter. As in the course of his flirtations he had evaded the final issue, the mother probably had employed some sorceress in order to ruin him. After an exchange of most comic letters this conjecture, too, had to be abandoned. One morning, however, when

Kovalyov awoke and glanced in the mirror, his nose had reappeared in its place as if nothing had happened. Kovalyov, feeling that he was himself once again, began to gallivant as before on the Nevsky Prospect, in the theatres and all sorts of other places. The nose 'sat on his face without the slightest hint that it had ever strayed in various directions.'

This phantasia on the sex-theme in disguise can be regarded as a *surréaliste* anticipation of the psycho-analytical symbolism of dreams applied to works of art. It may not appeal to the average reader, yet there is more method in its confusion than it might seem. Its plot abounds in amusing satire. And the bits of Petersburg life, whether bureaucratic or otherwise, add to the grotesqueness of the whole, especially when flavoured with Gogol's tone and accent. Here, too, his touch is as unmistakable as it is in *A Madman's Diary* or in his last Petersburg narrative, *The Greatcoat*.

6

The early draft of *The Greatcoat* goes back to the same period as the stories just discussed. It was actually begun by Gogol in 1839, under the anecdotal title, *The Official who Stole Overcoats*. During the next two years he remade it and gave it the present title. It was completed in 1841, and its final version came out in 1842, in the third volume of Gogol's collected works. The story is nearer to *A Madman's Diary* than to his other Petersburg tales. Its hero Akaky is a second Poprishchin, though older and more battered by life. He, too, is a copying-clerk, underpaid, humble, and sitting year after year at the same table, doing the same drudgery, as if he had been born into the world 'ready-made, as he was—uniform, bald patch and all.' He had become so used to his inferior social position that he did not even mind the younger clerks' cruel jeering at his expense. Only when their jokes were too crude would he react now and then, but feebly—like a sick animal which has been kicked and could arouse nothing but pity. Otherwise, Akaky was too much absorbed in his mechanical work to have time for anything else, least of all for his tormentors. He was even contented after a fashion, and would have remained so but for the vagaries of northern winters, against which his thin overcoat could no longer protect him. With some reluctance he consulted the eternally drunken tailor Petrovich. But the tailor refused to have anything to do with such a garment. He advised him to have a new coat made instead—a greatcoat, with marten collar, silver-plated buckles and all. Akaky first took it for a joke. But little by little the project got hold of him, until it became a fixed idea, a daydream he could no longer shake off. With endless privations he scraped together enough money to buy the necessary material. While doing this he felt elated, as though he had fallen in love. His prospective greatcoat was like a lover's vision of his sweetheart, or of a cherished wife. The greatcoat-theme is thus linked with Shponka's dream about his wife being made of woollen material. ' "What sort of stuff would you like?" asked the shopkeeper. "You had better take a wife that is of the most fashionable material! It wears well! Everyone is having coats made of it now!" The shopkeeper measured and cut off his wife. Ivan Fyodorovich Shponka put her under his arm and went off to a Jewish tailor.'

When the greatcoat was ready at last, Akaky was as happy as though a sweetheart or a wife had actually enriched his existence. Even the cat-skin (instead of marten) did not matter, for it had been so well chosen that from a distance it looked like marten. Anyway, on that memorable morning he walked into the office proudly, like a real somebody. There were shouts of surprise, of amazement, and his greatcoat became the topic of conversation. One of his superiors, who had a birthday-party on that very evening, decided to throw in the celebration of the greatcoat as well. So Akaky was duly invited. He came to the party, drank more than was good for him, and left the merry company rather late at night. But when—not without some trepidation—he was crossing a large, deserted square, a voice shouting, 'The greatcoat is mine,' sounded right in front of him, while someone seized him by the collar. Akaky opened his mouth to call for help, but a heavy fist sent him rolling to the ground. On regaining consciousness, he saw no trace either of his greatcoat or of the thieves. Mad with despair, he complained to the authorities, until a bureaucratic upstart—a 'person of consequence'—nearly frightened him out of his wits. In the end he fell mortally ill. But even in his delirium he kept talking of his beloved greatcoat and of the ruffians who had deprived him of it.

It should be stressed that this story, too, was spun from an anecdote which Gogol had heard at a tea-party in 1834. Someone mentioned the mishap of a minor official—a passionate sportsman who with his savings had bought a gun, but on the very first day of his hunting dropped it into the water, where it disappeared. The unlucky sportsman fell ill with despair and would probably have died, had not his colleagues made a collection and bought him another gun. In taking up this theme, Gogol disregarded—as in the anecdote about the two Ivans— its kindly human touch. He piled up a number of such trifles as were likely to turn Akaky into a pitiable parody of man, and the story itself into an indictment of life. Yet *The Greatcoat* is a literary masterpiece. Here Gogol builds up out of the most trivial details a character in whom misery, comedy and pathos seem to meet on equal terms. As if laughing at his own pity, the author makes the dying Akaky release some of his repressions by uttering oaths at which his old landlady crosses herself in horror. Then the story is rounded off with a joke about the defunct Akaky's 'ghost' stealing greatcoats at night in the streets of Petersburg—a reminiscence of the title given to the earlier draft of the story.

Although not the first to introduce the humble 'little man' into Russian fiction, Gogol was largely responsible for his literary canonization. He also rendered, in his own peculiar manner, that fantastically irrational yet, in its own way, real atmosphere of Petersburg which had been anticipated by Pushkin in *The Bronze Horseman* (1828) and *The Queen of Spades* (1833), and was later further developed by Dostoevsky. In his Petersburg stories Gogol's indictment of bureaucracy and of life as a whole came for the first time into its own. So did his moral pessimism. It was not long before the first reached its climax in his principal play *The Revizor,* and the second in his novel *Dead Souls.*

Chapter 6

Gogol the Playwright

1

As A BORN actor and impersonator, Gogol could not but see in the drama, or at least in the comedy, one of his natural mediums. Such a disposition made a temporary switch-over from stories to plays all the easier for him. As early as towards the end of 1832, that is, immediately after his first literary success, he began writing two comedies—*The Vladimir Order* and *The Wooers*—neither of which survived in its early shape. In the same year he was introduced by Sergei Aksakov to the famous Moscow actor, Shchepkin,[19] contact with whom may have served as a further incentive to playwriting.

Of the two plays Gogol was then engaged upon, *The Vladimir Order* was to be a satirical comedy, with a vain and dishonest official as its hero. Determined to obtain the Order of St Vladimir by fair means or foul, the official sees his ambitions thwarted by intrigues, until eventually he goes mad and begins to imagine that he himself is that Order. The theme offered a number of satirical possibilities, with jibes at the corrupt Tsarist bureaucracy, but Gogol was quick enough to realize that a comedy of this kind would never be allowed to appear either in print or on the stage. The hovering shadow of the censor made him give up his plan in despair.

'I did not mention to you the fact that I have gone crazy over the theme for a comedy,' he wrote to Professor M. P. Pogodin on 20th February 1833. 'It stuck in my mind all the time during my stay in Moscow, then on my journey and also after my return here, but nothing has come out of it so far. Not so long ago its content began to take shape, even its title was already gleaming on a sheet of paper, *The Vladimir Order of the Third Degree:* and how much malice, salt and laughter there was in it! . . . But I suddenly stopped when I saw that my pen began to stumble over utterances which the censor would never pass. What is the use of writing a play that has no chance of being performed, since it can live only on the stage? A play deprived of the stage is like a soul without a body. . . . The only thing to do is to write so as not to offend even the humblest police-sergeant. Yet what would a comedy be without truth and without malice?'

All that is left of the play are four satirical scenes, *The Morning of a Busy Man, A Lawsuit, The Servants' Hail* and simply *A Fragment*. These comic scenes were rewritten by Gogol and made independent of each other some time between 1837 and 1848. But the theme of the official who goes mad was not given up by him either. It reappeared in *A Madman's Diary*, where the hero of *The Vladimir Order* was split into two characters: Poprishchin and his exalted chief. Nor did Gogol's second planned comedy, *The Wooers*, remain without consequences. Having jotted it down in 1833, he took it up again later and published it in 1842 under the title *The Marriage*. In the meantime his dramatic talent reached its summit in *The Revizor* (*The Inspector-General*, or *The Government Inspector*), which is still regarded as the best satirical comedy in the Russian repertory.

2

Gogol started writing this play in October 1835 and finished it on 4th December of the same year—a record time for such a masterpiece. Much of the malice, irony and ridicule intended for his *Vladimir Order* came out in *The Revizor*, the laughter of which is so full of gall that audiences gasped when they first saw it on the stage. The play continued the Molièresque tradition in Russia, represented by such satirical comedies of manners as Fonvizin's *The Brigadier* and *The Minor*, Kapnist's *Chicane*, and Griboyedov's *Woe from Wit*. Its performance might have been postponed for years had not the poet Zhukovsky, the tutor to the heir apparent, read the manuscript and shown it to Nicholas I. The Tsar, who evidently was not always a fool, liked the comedy so much that, censors or no censors, he gave the order for its production at the Imperial Theatre without delay. The first performance took place on 19th April 1836[20] and—as was expected—created a furore. The Tsar himself, who was present, rocked with laughter and summed up his impressions by the phrase: 'Everyone has received his due, and I most of all.'

He did not exaggerate. Times and circumstances considered, *The Revizor* was a daring piece of work. The kind of laughter it aroused was by no means designed to please a ruler's ear or, for that matter, the ears of the officials so cruelly ridiculed. Yet the genesis of the play had been harmless enough. It all started with an anecdote of Pushkin's, how in 1833 he had been taken by some worthies at Nizhni Novgorod (now Gorky) for a high dignitary prowling round in order to find out all about the officials in those regions. Some further elements were gleaned by Gogol from Kvitka's *A Newcomer from the Capital*. This old-fashioned comedy of situation was written in 1827, but appeared in print only in 1840, that is, four years after *The Revizor*. As it contains several scenes reminiscent of the latter, the conclusion is that Gogol probably read it in manuscript. He may have also been acquainted with Corneille's *Le Menteur* and perhaps even with Goldoni's *Il Bugiardo* (*The Fibber*). But whatever the influences or borrowings, he made good use of them. Here he actually created the type of Russian liar—in the setting of remote provinces where defects and vices look even uglier and more grotesque that in reality. He also made use of a stronger condensation of characters, whereas the obligatory love-plot was abandoned by him, or rather, turned into a parody. The play itself, like Pushkin's anecdote from which it sprang, is based on the old-fashioned device of mistaken identity. Only in this case the officials of the distant provincial hole, and especially the *gorodnichy* or police-governor of the town, have more reasons than one to dread the Government Inspector who, according to some private intimation, is due to arrive from St Petersburg incognito and at any moment. In his panic, the *gorodnichy* summons the chief representatives of law and order and tells them what measures should be taken to make the town look at least moderately presentable. Intent on insuring himself against any denunciations, he has a heart-to-heart talk with the Postmaster Ivan Kuzmich.

GORODNICHY: Well, I'm not frightened, but I am a little uneasy about the tradespeople. They say they've found me difficult, though God's my judge, if I have taken from one or two, I did it without any ill-feeling (*Links arms with Postmaster and takes him aside*). I even think there may have been some secret denunciation of me. Why else should they send an Inspector here? Now, listen, Ivan Kuzmich, this is for our mutual benefit. Couldn't you take every letter that passes through your post office, and, well, just unseal it a little bit, you know, and read it through. Then if there was no denunciation or anything, you could reseal it somehow, or send it on unsealed.

POSTMASTER: I know, I know. . . . You're not teaching me anything. I've done it for years, not just as a precaution; I do like to know what goes on in the world. I tell you, it makes most interesting reading! And so edifying!

GORODNICHY: Have you found out anything about an official from Petersburg?

POSTMASTER: No! But plenty about those in Kostroma and Saratov. It's a pity you did not read the letters. Wonderful titbits! The other day a lieutenant wrote to a friend, describing a ball in most sprightly language, very, very nicely. 'My life, dear friend, soars to Empyrean heights of pleasure,' he wrote, 'young women, music, hard riding.' I kept it on purpose. Would you like to read it?

GORODNICHY: I can't be bothered now; but do me that favour, Ivan Kuzmich. If you find any complaint or denunciation, don't stop to think; keep it back.

POSTMASTER: I'll do that with pleasure.

Frightened as they are, the *gorodnichy* and his friends take for the dreaded Incognito a smartly dressed windbag, Khlestakov, who, together with his serf Osip, is travelling from Petersburg to his father's estate. Having lost all his money at cards, Khlestakov is practically starving at the local inn and waiting to be carted off to jail on account of his debt to the innkeeper. But here the *gorodnichy,* all a-tremble, pays a personal visit to him in order to find out whether Nemesis can still be averted through the magical expedient—bribery. They are both jittery at this first meeting: the magistrate because he knows what punishments are in store for him, supposing his mission to the 'Inspector' should not succeed; and Khlestakov, because he thinks at first that the *gorodnichy* has come to send him to jail. The young man is therefore quite beside himself with nerves and anger. He assumes an aggressive attitude, full of shouts and threats, all of which are interpreted by the panicky *gorodnichy* in his own way, i.e. as a sign of the 'Inspector's' displeasure with what he has already seen in the town. Hoping against hope that a substantial bribe—in the shape of a loan or on some other respectable pretext—may placate the furious 'Incognito,' the *gorodnichy* seizes the right moment, and with highly satisfactory results. The 'Incognito' is pacified and even persuaded to exchange his room at the inn for the *gorodnichy's* hospitable residence. Here he is feted and given further 'loans' by the trembling officials, all of whom are anxious to avert the castigating hand of justice. Khlestakov, on the other hand, finds himself in his right element. He piles one lie upon the other, swaggers to his heart's content, flirts with the hostess and in the end becomes 'betrothed' to the *gorodnichy's* daughter.

Yet it would be wrong to see in Khlestakov a schemer or even a conscious liar. He is too stupid for either. Irresponsible and spontaneous as a child, and much too vain—especially when drunk—to resist a display of his wishful grandeur before the overawed provincials, he is one of the most consummate *innocent* liars in literature, since he is always the first to believe everything he says. Like another Poprishchin, he needs an imaginary compensation for his actual insignificance, and he finds it in bragging like a megalomaniac. No exaggeration is too much for him as long as he can revel with gusto in all he thinks he is, and make other people think so too. His house is the grandest in Petersburg. There he gives balls and dinners, the magnificence of which surpasses all description.

Now, for instance, I might have on the table . . . a . . . a watermelon that cost me 700 roubles. (*Gasps from the company*). And the soup brought on a fast steamer straight from Paris! And the aroma as soon as you lift the lid! Incomparable! I go to balls every day. When we're bored with dancing, we may make up a four at whist, the Foreign Minister, the French Ambassador, the English Ambassador, the German Ambassador and I.

Khlestakov is so naive indeed that he does not see through the *gorodnichy's* 'hospitality.' But his serf Osip is an astute enough rascal to guess that the good folk in the town have taken his master for someone more important. So he persuades him to say good-bye before it is too late. His tipsy head full of pleasant memories and his pockets bulging with money, Khlestakov departs, amidst cheers, 'for a day or two'—under the pretext of bringing back his father's blessing for the forthcoming marriage. No sooner has the 'Inspector' gone than the *gorodnichy*, puffed up with success and with the prospect of having such a son-in-law, begins to display his own self-importance with a vengeance. He is particularly hard on the tradespeople who dared to lodge a complaint against him in spite of the precautions he had taken to prevent anything of the sort. When he reproaches them, his anger assumes even the tone of moral indignation because of their ungratefulness.

'And who showed you how to make a fortune on that bridge contract, when you put the timber down at 20,000 roubles and it was not worth a hundred! I helped you, goat-beard! And I can also send you to Siberia! What about that? . . .'

But his interview with the merchants ends in a conciliatory mood.

'Well, God pardons all! I don't bear malice. But see it doesn't happen again. I'm marrying my daughter soon, but not to any petty landowner! Congratulations are in order, you understand! And they'd better be substantial! None of your dried fish and sugar-loaves! Well, God be wi' you!'

As in the meantime the news of his daughter's betrothal has spread in the town, his home is buzzing with visitors anxious to congratulate the mighty man. The parents of the happy bride-to-be strut condescendingly about, while their thoughts are already in far-away Petersburg. The *gorodnichy* and his wife are in fact so sure of their future grandeur in the capital that they can no longer resist showing open contempt for their provincial friends and acquaintances. Suddenly the Postmaster, nervous and distraught, comes in waving a letter. Acting on the *gorodnichy's* instructions, he has, with great fear and reluctance, opened the letter posted by Khlestakov himself.

POSTMASTER: Well, so help me God, I opened it! I've never been so terrified in my life! I shut the shutters, locked the door, blocked the keyhole, and broke the seals with my own hand. And when I touched the wax, fire ran in my veins, my body felt on fire. And when I unsealed it, frost surged over me.

GORODNICHY: But how dared you open the mail of such an important personage?

POSTMASTER: But that's just it! He isn't important and he isn't a personage. He wasn't the Inspector-General.

GORODNICHY: Well, since you know so much, what is he?

POSTMASTER: Neither one thing nor the other. The devil only knows who he is.

GORODNICHY (*angrily*): What do you mean? How dare you speak of him like that? I shall arrest you.

POSTMASTER: Who? You?

GORODNICHY: Yes, Me!

POSTMASTER: You couldn't even if you tried!

GORODNICHY: Do you know he's going to marry my daughter? I shall be a Petersburg grandee then, and I'll have you sent to Siberia.

POSTMASTER (*nervously*): Eh! Siberia! It's a long way off, you know, Siberia! But I'd better read the letter. May I?

ALL: Read it! Read it!

POSTMASTER: My dear Tryapichkin![21] I must write and tell you about my marvellous adventures lately. I told you how I got cleaned out by an infantry captain at Penza; well, I finally got stranded here. The innkeeper-fellow wanted to send me to jail. I didn't write to the old man; he is furious with me, told me never to ask him for another kopek. Well, suddenly, owing I suppose to my Petersburg clothes and distinguished-looking face, the whole of this blessed town took me for the Governor-General. And now I am living in the *gorodnichy's* house, having the time of my life, and carrying on desperate flirtations with his wife and daughter. My only trouble is, I can't decide which to go for first. I think, the old lady; she seems to be ready for anything. Do you remember when we were both hard up, and the pastrycook threw me out of the shop for charging my pies to the King of England? Well, it's quite different now. Everybody presses money into my hand; always as loans, of course. Frightful half-wits. You'd die laughing! First there's the *gorodnichy:* he's a generous chap, his hospitality is like a pole-axe, but he's as stupid as an old grey mule. . . .

The same strain pervades the rest of the letter. Each member of the bureaucratic confraternity is regaled with an appropriate zoological epithet. And the effect is worse than that of a thunderbolt. The *gorodnichy's* wrath knows no limits. But when the general consternation is at its height the doors fly open. In comes a gendarme and, standing to attention, addresses the *gorodnichy*:

'His Excellency the Inspector-General appointed by Imperial decree has arrived from St. Petersburg. He is in residence at the hotel, and requires your presence there immediately.'

The curtain slowly falls, the varied attitudes of the actors expressing the fright, wonder, horror and stupefaction of the whole company.

3

With its motif, its wealth of character and incident, *The Revizor* stands out as a satirical comedy of the highest rank. Belinsky saw in it a promise of the eagerly awaited renewal of the theatre in Russia whose repertory still consisted either of vaudevilles and melodramas (largely imported from abroad), or of gushing patriotic plays manufactured by Gogol's schoolfellow Kukolnik and others. Judged by any standards, the general level of the Russian theatre of that period was poor. This made *The Revizor* all the more welcome—to the discerning few. Here at last was a contemporary comedy as good as it could be; a piece in which every *dramatis persona* had definite features and even an individual language of his own. Even the social sting contained in it is not imposed, but comes as it were from within, from the subject-matter itself. And since the characters remain to the end at that subhuman level at which vices and abuses are regarded as something normal (provided one is not caught), the irony of the comedy is often in the very 'innocence' with which the officials talk about their transgressions and, without knowing it, whip themselves by their naive candour. One of the worthies, for example, is upbraided by the *gorodnichy* not for taking bribes, but because he takes them 'above his rank.' The gap between their own standpoint and that of the author is filled with Gogol's laughter at its loudest and most typical. Several years later, when Gogol tried to evaluate his play retrospectively, he wrote apropos of it in his *Confession of an Author:* 'I saw that in my former works I laughed for nothing, uselessly, without knowing why. If it is necessary to laugh, then why not laugh at what deserves to be ridiculed by us all? In my *Revizor* I decided to gather in one focus and to deride all that is bad in Russia, all the evils perpetrated in those places where the utmost rectitude is required of man.' Elsewhere (in his *Homegoing from the Theatre*) he enlarges upon the same idea by saying: 'If comedy must be a picture and a mirror of our social life, then let it reflect it in all its truth.' And this brings us again to the problem of Gogol's realism, as well as to the impulse that lay behind it. In obeying that impulse, he did not copy the truth, but showed it in a crooked mirror. Only by exaggerating it could he give such a slap to reality as to satisfy both his romantic and his moral rancour. For, needless to say, it is not so much Gogol's social as his moral pathos that rings out between the lines of his indictments.

This subjective aspect remained hidden from the public. What the audience saw in *The Revizor* was a burlesque, a farce, a distorted picture of Russian life, and above all an impertinent attack on the entire bureaucratic and autocratic system of Russia. Whereas the liberal-minded spectators could not but approve of it, the representatives of the official world were beside themselves with fury. A hue and cry was raised against the 'unpatriotic' author by those he had lampooned. But for the Tsar's tolerant attitude towards the play, things might have turned out rather unpleasantly for Gogol. Indeed, he soon found them unpleasant enough for him to shake the dust of Russia off his feet, and this time in all earnest. 'A contemporary author who writes comedies of manners should live as far from his own country as possible,' he reasoned in a letter to Pogodin. 'No prophet can earn glory in his native land. I don't mind that all classes of society have risen against me; still, it is sad and depressing to see my country-men, whom I sincerely love, attack me so unjustly, and interpret everything in such a perverted fashion.'

So without further ado Gogol left at the beginning of June 1836 for Western Europe, where he stayed until 1848. During all that time he only went back to Russia on two occasions. It was abroad, mostly in Rome, that he finished his *Dead Souls*. It was abroad also that he resumed the theme of his *Wooers*, a rewritten version of which, under the title *The Marriage*, he had sent to Pushkin in the autumn 1835, that is, several months before he left Russia. Whatever Pushkin's verdict of that early version may have been, Gogol continued to work on it while at Rome. It was first published in 1842 and is now generally acknowledged as Gogol's second-best play.

4

The subject matter of *The Marriage*, too, points to an anecdotal origin. This time Gogol was concerned primarily with fun, much of which is lost on those Western readers or listeners who are not acquainted with the old Russian custom of marriages arranged by professional match-makers. In Gogol's days this *métier* was still in full swing. Impoverished gentlemen, who had turned officials or simply gone to seed, were always on the look-out for merchants' daughters with big dowries. In many merchant-families, again, there was enough snobbery left to make them wish to see their daughters married to noblemen even of a seedy kind. Gogol, with his penchant for that burlesque mix-up of situations in which people turn into their own parodies, saw in an encounter between the two strata plenty of material for a comedy of manners. The more so because it gave him an opportunity to treat wedlock itself as a mere commercial contract in which the dowry is of far greater importance than its appendage, the bride.

As it happens, Gogol's matchmaker Thekla (an excellent portrait!) has collected some six pretenders to the hand of the merchant's daughter Agafya—all of them mere 'existers' of whom the respectable civil servant Podkolyosin has the best chance. Podkolyosin belongs, however, to the same undersexed category as Shponka in *Evenings*, and it is here that the fun begins. The difference between Shponka and Podkolyosin is that the latter is divided between his strong wish to be married and his equally strong fear of such a condition. He indulges in the dreams of wedded bliss, while on the other hand he remains reluctant to commit himself entirely even after his friend, the hot-headed busy-body Kochkaryov (the conventional fuss-pot and one of Thekla's old victims), has taken on the duty of matchmaker. Thanks to his friend's endeavours, things have advanced so far that, in spite of periodical fits of panic, Podkolyosin is about to lead Agafya to the altar. He waits in her house, while she dresses for the great occasion. Having bestowed his first kiss on her plump cheeks, he grows most enthusiastic about marriage. But his subconscious fear of it still keeps preying on him. The conflict between the two dispositions ends with a quite incredible happening, which can best be explained by Podkolyosin's own soliloquy as his bride is getting ready in the next room.

'What have I been till now, in reality? Did I understand the significance of life? I didn't. I understood nothing. What, what has my bachelor existence been like? What was I good for? What did I do? I went on from day to day, did my work, went to the office, ate my dinner, and went to sleep—in fact, I've been the most frivolous and ordinary man in the world. Only now one sees how silly every one is who doesn't get married; yet if you come to think of it, what a number of men go on living in blindness. If I were a king, I would order everyone to be married! All at once will taste bliss such as is only to be found in fairy tales, which there's no expressing, nor finding words to express, indeed. (*After a pause*). But, say what you will, it is positively alarming when one thinks it over. To bind oneself for all one's life, for all one's days, come what may, and no getting out of it afterwards, no retracting it, nothing, nothing—everything over, everything settled. Why, even now it is impossible to turn back; in another minute I shall be in church; it is quite impossible to get away—there's the carriage there already and everything prepared. But is it really impossible to get away? Why, of course, it's im-

possible. There are people standing there, and at the door
and everywhere. Why, they'll ask what for? I cannot. No.
But there's the window open. What about the window?
No, I can't; why, to be sure it's unseemly; besides, it's a
long way from the ground. . . . (*Goes up to the window*)
Oh well, it's not so high; there's only the one storey, and
that's a low one. Oh no, how could I: I haven't even a cap.
How can I go without a hat? What if I were to try, eh?
Shall I try? (*Stands on the window and saying* Lord help
he! *jumps into the street; is heard moaning and groaning
below*). Oh, it was a long way, though. Hi, cabman!'

He probably escapes with a broken rib, but this may still be
a lesser calamity for him than marriage. The farcical *vaudeville*
element is thus apparent. But light though the play is on the
surface, its structure is very compact; its pace is swift, and its
dialogue racy and idiomatic enough to defy even the best translators. As for the characters, their *typicality* is as emphatic as in
The Revizor, but they are drawn without rancour. The scene
where the phlegmatic Podkolyosin is forcibly dragged by his
friend to Agafya's house, and there finds five other competitors,
is particularly funny. Gogol's puns, jokes and allusions may at
times be on the coarse side, but this is partly in keeping with
the nature of the theme itself. There is comicality also in the
names of the characters; in Gogol's frequent interpolation of
seemingly irrelevant trifles; and finally in the very accent of the
repartees. In spite of its jocularity, this play is even more difficult to act than *The Revizor* (its first performance in Petersburg on 9th December 1842 was in fact a failure). But in the
hands of a competent producer it can keep the audience rocking
with laughter from the first scene to the last.

5

Gogol's other dramatic ventures can be dealt with briefly,
since the only two finished achievements among them are
Homegoing from the Theatre and the one-act play *The Gam-*

blers. The first of them was jotted down in 1836, but he finished it in 1842, obviously in emulation of Molière's *La Critique de l'Ecole des Femmes.* It can be regarded as a successful attempt at self-criticism put into the mouths of the various spectators going home after a performance of *The Revizor.* It is a vivid and shrewdly observed piece of work, in which the voice of Gogol the moralist has already gathered in volume. His two other exclusively moralizing fragments, *The Denouement of The Revizor* (1846) and an *Addition to the Denouement of The Revizor* (1847), have no dramatic value and therefore need not detain us here. As for *The Gamblers,* its first draft may have been made before 1836, but its present form dates from 1840-42. Based on cleverly manipulated suspense and mystification, it has a finale as striking for the spectators as it is for the cheated cheat—the hero of the play. Like *The Revizor,* it has not a single positive character. Another of its features is that it contains male parts only.

It may be of some interest that in 1835 Gogol started a tragedy from English history, but all that remains of it are a few jottings under the title *Alfred.* They are feeble enough to prove that writing tragedies was not his vocation. Another excursion into history was made by him in 1839-40, when he was busy with a romantic Cossack drama 'of the Taras Bulba type,' but with the strangest of titles, *The Shaved Moustache.* In September 1841 he read to Zhukovsky what he had written. As the tired poet fell asleep during the process, Gogol was so much annoyed that he threw the manuscript into the fire.

The reputation of Gogol the playwright thus rests primarily on *The Revizor.* And the effect this comedy had on the Russian audiences was one of the factors responsible for his change towards art in general. Prior to its performance in 1836 he was still groping, as it were, in various directions for his true life-work. The character of his *Arabesques* shows that he must have been vacillating, now and then, between literature proper and his quasi-scientific, pedagogic and preaching inclinations. That was the time when he planned also a history of the Ukraine, then a world-history, or at least a history of the Middle Ages—

'in eight or perhaps nine volumes.' *The Revizor* put an end to his uncertainty. The impression it had made on the stage was enough to fan in Gogol the idea that he was a moral castigator whose duty it was not only to ridicule human vices and combat evil by means of laughter, but also to direct men on to the path of light and virtue. In the very animosities aroused by *The Revizor* he was inclined to see a proof that divine Providence was using, or intended to use, his pen and talent for some higher purposes which were beyond the ken of ordinary mortals. 'It is not an earthly Will that guides me,' he modestly wrote to Pletnyov in 1836. From that time on, this delusion kept growing in him, and, for a number of years, even acted as a source of inspiration. Indeed it was at least partly responsible for the character of his greatest and most mature work, the novel *Dead Souls*.

Chapter 7

Dead Souls

1

THE YEARS during which Gogol concentrated his energies on *Dead Souls* were also the years of his most restless roamings and wanderings. But the urge to travel was a passion with him, almost an obsession; as if he were engaged in an eternal flight from himself, or from some invisible foes he was unable to escape. On the other hand, this was a condition, or rather a state of mind, which he regarded as necessary for his creative process. 'My head is so queerly constituted that there are times when I must suddenly leave behind me a few hundred miles and run through all that distance in order to replace one impression by another, to clear my mind's eye, and to gather enough strength for the tasks I have to accomplish.' Thus he wrote to Shevyryov in 1843. Now and then he even tried to justify (not very convincingly) such a habit by the idea that he had to know the whole of Europe in order better to understand those aspects of Russian life which he wanted to tackle in his future works. Anyway, the distance, the 'long, long road,' proved in the end so irresistible that he simply could not stop in one place, unless he interrupted his stay by periodic excursions. As if driven by his own demon of restlessness, he had to go on and on. And the longer he travelled the more he wanted to travel.

A catalogue of all the places he visited or stayed in on leaving Russia in 1836 would make a long list, if it could be compiled at all. Suffice it to say that from Petersburg he went to Vevey in Switzerland, where he stayed for a while, and then to Paris. In March 1837 he settled in Rome. But in the summer of the same year we find him at Baden-Baden, where he met his old acquaintance, now Madame Rosset-Smirnova, for whom he had contracted a peculiar, old-maidish kind of attachment. After that he lived mostly in Rome until September 1839, when he visited Petersburg and Moscow. In the summer of 1840 we find him in Vienna, then again in Rome. In March of the following year he left for Germany and later once more for Russia. In May 1842 he went to Austria, from Austria to Munich, from Munich to Rome, from Rome to Florence, from Florence to Germany, whence he returned again to Rome. The month of January 1845 he spent in Paris (with Count Vielgorsky's family), and less than a year later he was in Germany. At the beginning of 1848 he made a journey to Palestine, after which he settled in Moscow—from now on his centre. But in Russia, too, he continued roaming. Unable to come to terms either with himself or with life, he was doomed to travel—as if hoping to find in new places what he had missed in the old ones. His urge to travel was in fact both a quest and a flight.

There was one place, however, which he really loved and where he felt more at home than anywhere else. This place was Rome. 'You fall in love with Rome slowly, little by little—and for the rest of your life,' Gogol wrote to one of his friends. 'In short, Europe exists in order to watch, and Italy in order to live.' An expression of his enthusiasm was his fragment *Rome*,[22] otherwise a much too rhetorical beginning of a planned novel (*Annunziata*) about Italian life, or rather about the Eternal City which never ceased to fascinate him. What appealed to him in particular was its picturesque medieval flavour, its romantic unreality and remoteness from anything 'modern.' And no wonder. New ideas, the social and political struggles that were brewing in those days in Italy and in the rest of Europe, were so alien to Gogol that he could never grasp them. Nor was his cultural equipment solid enough to enable him to take a broader interest in Western civilization as such. His friend P. V. Annenkov[23] says (in his *Gogol in Rome*) that the only foreign author some of whose works Gogol knew at the time was Sir Walter Scott. Shakespeare he had hardly read at all, while his knowledge of Goethe and other great figures in the republic of letters was equally scant. In the same work Annenkov stresses Gogol's patriarchal-romantic propensity to cling only to what was old and time-honoured: 'It was noticeable that the loss of some ancient custom, even if suspected by him as being due to new currents, struck him unpleasantly. He was in love with his own conception of Rome, and herein he was partly influenced by the Ukrainian element in him which always looks for the signs of old times and for reminiscences of the past.'

Be this as it may, he found—especially during his early years abroad—intense pleasure in the very atmosphere of Rome and in the Italian setting in general. 'With what relief I gave up Switzerland and flew to my sweetheart, to my beauty—Italy,' he wrote after his first impression of the Papal City. 'She is mine! No one will take her from me. This is my real birth-place. Russia, Petersburg, snows, scoundrels, departments, the University-chair, the theatre—all this was but a dream. Now I have awakened in my true homeland. The mighty hand of Providence has flung me beneath the glittering sky of Italy with a special aim as it were—that I should forget my worries, forget everything, and cling only to her beauty. She has now replaced all, as far as I am concerned.' In Rome, the southerner awoke in Gogol, and he recovered at least that amount of serenity and gaiety of which he was still capable. From that 'lovely, far-away paradise' he now threw a critical glance at his own country and proceeded to write his novel, *Dead Souls,* which (after many difficulties with the censors) was to appear in Moscow in 1842 under the revised title, *The Adventures of Chichikov or Dead Souls.*

2

The first two chapters of this masterpiece had been jotted down by Gogol in the autumn of 1835. Judging by a letter he had sent to Pushkin on 7th October of the same year, he wanted to show in his novel 'the whole of Russia at least from one of her angles.' And once more it was Pushkin who had given him the idea.[24] Pushkin himself may have had in mind writing a narrative of this sort, but he evidently ceded the theme to Gogol, even though he once referred to him as 'that sly Ukrainian, capable of robbing you before you have time to cry for help.' Yet Pushkin was the first to admire the drafts that Gogol read to him while still in Petersburg. He laughed heartily—so Gogol says; but soon his face grew gloomy, and he could not help exclaiming: 'Lord, what a sad country our Russia is!' It is possible that Gogol's first intention was just an amusing satirical novel. During the progress of composition, however, the subject-matter kept both deepening and expanding, until its canvas began to assume much bigger proportions than he had perhaps expected. 'I am again busy with my *Dead Souls,* which I began in Petersburg,' he announced in December 1836 in a letter to Zhukovsky from Paris. 'I have rewritten all that I had done before. Having reconsidered the whole plan, I am now working it out quietly, as if it were a chronicle. . . . If I ever complete this work in the manner I want to, what a colossal and original theme it will be! What a varied crowd of characters! The whole of Russia will appear in it! This will be the first product of mine that will preserve my name.'

The structure of *Dead Souls* does not essentially deviate from that of the picaresque novel. Its literary relatives are *Don Quixote, Gil Blas,* and also *The Pickwick Papers,* not to mention the more superficial didactic-satirical novels of adventure as practised in Russia by Narezhny and Bulgarin.[25] This means that its chapters are above all a string of episodes connected through the exploits of a travelling, up-to-date substitute for the *picaro,* i.e. the adventurer or the rogue. And since Cervantes had originally called his great book an epic, Gogol too styled *Dead Souls* not a novel but an epic (in Russian—*poema*). Its pattern, however, is much less involved than that of *Don Quixote,* and is without even a love-story. Whereas in both *The Revizor* and *The Marriage* Gogol parodies love, in *Dead Souls* he just leaves it out. This makes the plot even less exciting. On the other hand, the centre of gravity rests throughout on the characters and their setting, depicted (as in *The Old-World Landowners*) with the minuteness of the Dutch School and interspersed with comments, or with descriptive, lyrical and didactic digressions of which Gogol is never chary. What is thus likely to strike the reader is the absence of anything really 'striking.' The Gogol of the ultra-romantic period—*A Horrid Vengeance, Viy,* or the picturesque *Taras Bulba*—has now been left behind. What he presents in *Dead Souls* is an artistic image of life in its everyday tedium, vulgarity and drabness, but condensed and intensified as only Gogol knew how. If taken on the surface only, the method is realistic. Yet, as in *The Greatcoat,* Gogol disintegrates as it were the reality he deals with into its innumerable details and *petits faits,* after which he modifies, retouches and changes all the proportions according to his own subjective vision of human existence. The drab mediocrity of life, presented through the characters and their background, is revealed by him, step by step, in all its senselessness. Here it is not the exceptions, but the respectable average, with its grotesquely comic antics and with that panorama of life's humdrum whose tragedy consists in its very inability to be tragic, that begins to haunt the reader's imagination. The introduction of the principal hero himself is devoid of any spectacular happenings, when in a chaise driven by a *troika* (a team of three horses) he and his two servants arrive in a sleepy provincial town.

In the chaise sat a gentleman neither handsome but not bad looking, not too stout and not too thin; it could not be said that he was old, neither could he be described as very young. His arrival in the town created no sensation whatever, and was not accompanied by anything remarkable.

The newcomer, Pavel Ivanovich Chichikov, is himself a respectable average 'gentleman of the middling sort.' Gogol spares no details in order to bring out precisely this characteristic. He makes us follow Chichikov to his room at the local inn and watch him how he dresses, eats, chats with the waiter and drives out to pay his respects to the local potentates, such as the governor of the province, the police inspector and others. We learn in the course of his visits that he is also modest and reticent about his own person. When he feels he must say something about himself, he only makes a few discreet remarks to the effect that he has suffered from his enemies for the sake of Right and that he is on the look-out for some peaceful corner where he can settle down. At the governor's evening-party, to which he has been invited, he charms all and sundry by his manners, consummate tact and adroitness in conversation.

Whatever the subject of conversation, he could always keep it up: was horse-breeding discussed, he talked about horse-breeding; if they conversed about the best dogs, on that subject too he made very apt observations; if they touched on a case inquired into by the court of justice, he showed that he was not ignorant of court procedure; if the topic was a game of billiards, he was not at sea in billiards either; if the conversation turned upon virtue, he made excellent reflections upon virtue, and even with tears in his eyes; if upon the preparation of hot punch, he was an authority on punch too; if upon overseers of the customs and excise-officers, he discoursed about them as though he had been himself an excise-officer or an overseer of the customs. But it was noteworthy that he succeeded in accompanying all this with a certain sedateness, and knew very well how to behave. He spoke neither too loudly nor too low, but exactly as he ought. Take him how you would, he was a thoroughly gentlemanly man.

So much for Chichikov's façade. Little by little we are taken behind that genteel appearance and learn, not without a shock, that he is engaged in a series of transactions of a somewhat shady kind. What he is after is nothing less than 'buying up' a number of fictitious, that is, deceased, serfs (or *souls* as they were called in Russia), whose deaths had not yet been registered by the census. As the census of serfs took place only every ten years, Chichikov devised the plan of mortgaging the bought-up 'dead souls' who were officially still regarded as alive. With the money thus realized he hoped to settle in some distant part of Russia, where no one would be able to find out anything about his past. The district chosen by him for such strange exploits had just been through a severe epidemic, and the 'peasants had died, thank goodness, in great numbers.' So his prospects looked rosy enough, even if he omitted, in the course of his transaction, one or two items of vital importance. Thus Aksakov pointed out in a letter to Gogol (on 3rd July 1842) that serfs bought with the purpose of being transferred elsewhere could only be sold together with their families, whereas Chichikov refused to buy women.

3

Having been introduced to a few local landowners, Chichikov wastes no time and sets out to try his luck on them. The manner in which Gogol renders their portraits has often been compared with that of Dickens. He too, like Dickens, shows his characters not in their process of growth and development but as finished types, with all their habitual *tics*. Like Dickens again, Gogol is fond of comic or even burlesque caricatures. But the comic element in Dickens shows a benevolent if often indignant attitude towards life, whereas in Gogol, as in Hogarth, it expresses spite and hidden disgust. Here Gogol's comic figures are even suggestive of the more solid, three-dimensional art of Brueghel. Their external features not only reflect their inner selves, but fit most perfectly into their surroundings as well. Adroit as he is, Chichikov handles the landowners with his customary tact and shrewdness. His first transaction with the sugary, sentimental fool Manilov has most satisfactory results. With other landowners, such as the crafty country-bear Sobakevich, the stingy, half-witted but cunning dame Korobochka, or the eternal cheat, scandal-monger and *ami cochon* Nozdryov, things do not proceed so smoothly. His greatest success is scored, however, with that 'tatter of humanity'—the miser Plyushkin. And since the characters, portrayed here, are types representing entire categories of human beings, they live with a convincingness of their own which is enhanced by their automatic habits and gestures.

Sobakevich, for example, is all matter and materialism, oozing with a heavy, clumsily solid animality.

When Chichikov stole a sidelong glance at Sobakevich, he struck him on this occasion as being extremely like a middle-sized bear. To complete the resemblance, his dress-coat was precisely the colour of bear's skin, his sleeves were long, his trousers were long, he ambled from side to side as he walked and was continually treading on other people's feet. His face was burnt as dark red as a copper penny. We all know that there are in the world a great many faces on the carving of which nature has spent no great pains, has used no delicate tools such as files or gimlets, but has simply rough-hewn them with a swing of the arm: one stroke of the axe and there's a nose, another and there are the lips; the eyes are bored with a great drill; and without polishing it off nature thrusts it into the world, saying: 'This will do.' Just such an uncouth and strangely-hewn countenance was that of Sobakevich: he held it rather drooping than erect, he did not turn his neck at all, and in consequence of his immobility he rarely looked at the person to whom he was speaking, but always stared away at the corner of the stove or at the door. Chichikov stole another glance at him as they reached the dining-room; he was a bear, a regular bear, and to complete the strange resemblance his name was actually Mikhail Semyonovich.[26]

Nozdryov, again, was a 'historical' character in the sense that no gathering at which he was present ever ended without a 'history,' i.e. a row or scandal. As an incurable gambler and card-sharper, he was not a stranger to certain tricks which invariably landed him in disputes of such violence that he often returned home with one whisker only instead of two.

And what is strangest of all, and only possible in Russia, within a short time he would meet again the very friends who have given him such a dressing, and meet them as though nothing had happened: he, as the saying is, did not turn a hair, and they did not turn a hair.

The most unforgettable of Gogol's portraits is, however, that of the miser Plyushkin. When Chichikov first saw him, he could not even decide whether the face before him was that of an old man or of an old woman. Nor could he make out, for all his scrutiny, what material Plyushkin's costume, or rather dressing-gown, was made of.

> The sleeves and the upper part of the skirts were so greasy and shiny that they looked like the polished leather of which high boots are made; at the back instead of two there were four tails out of which cotton wool hung in tufts! Then there was something round his neck, too, which it was impossible to identify: it might have been a stocking, or a bandage, or a stomach-belt, but it certainly could not be a cravat.

No matter whether Gogol deals with single landowners or whole assemblies of officialdom and town-society, the undertone of his pages intimates something that goes beyond mere realism and imparts to his accumulation of trifles a symbolic meaning. He himself once hurled at his critics the remark: 'Those who have dissected my literary abilities were not able to find out the essential features of my nature. Only Pushkin was able to do it. He always asserted that no other author had such a capacity for bringing out all the trivialities of life, of describing so well the vulgarity of the mediocre man and life.' Chichikov himself is the embodiment of smug, conventional mediocrity, always on the look-out for gain and comfort. The disinterested liar Khlestakov is a child in comparison with this sedate gentleman who trades in 'dead souls' and swindles with the most impeccable drawing-room manners. Mediocrity and vulgarity were thus identical in Gogol's mind, and their diluted, ubiquitous essence seemed to him most ineradicable when decked in respectable appearances. Here more than anywhere else Gogol's laughter and irony became a fight against what he understood by the devil, or the evil element latent in life. 'For a long time I have been preoccupied with one thing: how to make a man who has read my works have his fill of laughter over the devil,' he said, rather significantly, in a letter to Shevyryov.[27] The comical characters parading in *Dead Souls* may cause a great deal of laughter. For all that the final impression they make is not one of gaiety but of sadness; of that ethical sadness which arises from our suspicion that something is wrong with life at its root, in its very essence. Gogol's mastery is here measured above all by the skill with which he brings out the moral and spiritual world of their characters simply by describing their external features. Moreover, he has found a short cut to the 'psychology' of the landowners in the way that each of them reacts to Chichikov's delicate commercial proposition. We thus obtain not only repeated glimpses of Chichikov's business acumen, but also of the stuff his clients are made of. Sobakevich's reaction is a case in point, and the deliberately long-winded style employed here only emphasizes the tortuous character of the situation itself.

Sobakevich bent his head slightly, and prepared to hear what the business might be. Chichikov approached the subject indirectly, touched on the Russian empire in general, and spoke with great appreciation of its vast extent, said that even the ancient Roman empire was not so vast, and that foreigners may well marvel at it. . . . (Sobakevich still listened with his head bowed), and that in accordance with the existing ordinances of the government, whose fame had no equal, souls on the census-list who had ended their earthly career were, until the next census was taken, reckoned as though they were alive, in order to avoid burdening the government departments with a multitude of petty and unimportant details and increasing the complexity of the administrative machinery, complicated as it is. . . . (Sobakevich still listened with his head bowed), and that, justifiable as this arrangement was, it yet put a somewhat heavy burden on many landowners, compelling them to pay the tax as though for living serfs, and that through a sentiment of personal respect for him, he was prepared to some extent to relieve him of his burdensome obligation. In regard to the real subject of his remarks, Chichikov expressed himself very cautiously, and never spoke of the souls as dead, but invariably as non-existent. Sobakevich still listened as before with his head bent, and not a trace of anything approaching expression showed on his face. It seemed as though in that body there was no soul at all, or if there was that it was not in its proper place, but, as with the immortal Boney, somewhere far away and covered with so thick a shell that whatever was stirring at the bottom of it produced not the faintest ripple on the surface.

'And so . . . ?' said Chichikov, waiting, not without some perturbation, for an answer.

'You want the dead souls?' inquired Sobakevich very simply, with no sign of surprise, as though they had been talking of corn.

'Yes,' said Chichikov, and again he softened the expression, adding, 'non-existent ones.'

'There are some; to be sure there are,' said Sobakevich.

'Well, if you have any, you will doubtless be glad to get rid of them?'

'Certainly, I am willing to sell them,' said Sobakevich, slightly raising his head, and reflecting that doubtless the purchaser would make some profit out of them.

'Deuce take it!' thought Chichikov to himself. 'He is ready to sell them before I drop a hint of it.' And aloud he said:

'And what is the price, for instance? Though, indeed it is a queer sort of goods . . . it seems odd to speak of the price.'

With other landowners other tricks are required, but it is sagacity that comes to Chichikov's rescue. His very politeness assumes different shades, or even disappears entirely, according to the nature of the person he is dealing with. He does not stand on ceremony with such a dense specimen as Madame Koro-bochka. Nor does he pay attention to diplomatic niceties in his encounter with Nozdryov, although here, for the first time, he feels completely lost and it is only by chance that he escapes from being regaled with a severe drubbing. Each chapter of *Dead Souls* thus has a climax of its own. But they all converge in such a manner as to make Chichikov's sudden downfall almost as unavoidable as was the downfall of the *gorodnichy* in *The Revizor*.

4

It all happened in accordance with the law of cause and effect. While Pavel Ivanovich Chichikov was doing his round of visits among the landowners of the district, rumours about his wealth began to spread among the townfolk. Some good people would have it that he was nothing less than a millionaire —a real millionaire buying up serfs for cash in order to settle them on his newly-acquired estate somewhere in the south— in the Kherson district, as he himself had vaguely hinted. Nor did the word 'millionaire' in this case lose any of its attraction. Added to Chichikov's polished manners, it seemed to have hypnotized most of the town. The ladies, in the first place, found him so irresistible that they exhausted all their wits and their husbands' purses in order to outstrip one another in toilettes they wanted to scintillate in at the forthcoming ball in the Governor's palace, to which—as they all knew—Chichikov had been invited. Chichikov actually came. And no sooner had he entered the hall than he and not the Governor was the centre of attention.

'Pavel Ivanovich!' 'Ah goodness me, Pavel Ivanovich!' 'Dear Pavel Ivanovich!' 'Oh, here you are, Pavel Ivanovich!' . . . There was no end of joyful exclamations. The ladies were even more astir, and continued to vie for his favour even after he had lingered much too long in the company of the Governor's pretty daughter. In short, all of them tried to be within or near the radiance emanating from him. But when this general adulation was at its height, Nozdryov suddenly put in an appearance. To make things worse, he was already tipsy, and therefore in more than his usual high spirits. At the very moment when the Governor was asking our 'precious Pavel Ivanovich' to arbitrate between him and two ladies as to whether love was constant, Nozdryov ran up to his Excellency and, turning to Chichikov, went off into a guffaw.

'Ah, the Kherson landowner! The Kherson landowner! Well, have you bought a lot of dead souls? I expect you don't know, your Excellency (he bawled, addressing the Governor), he deals in dead souls! Upon my word! I say, Chichikov! Let me tell you, I may say it as a friend, we are all your friends here, and here is his Excellency too— I'd hang you, upon my soul I would . . .'

The effect can be imagined. Although no one ever took Nozdryov's words seriously, Chichikov had plenty of reasons for feeling uneasy. A cloud began to gather over his social success, and suspicions once aroused could not be allayed. Rumours about 'dead souls' threw the local gossips into an orgy of guesses and speculations. Chichikov soon began to intrigue them as a puzzling, mysterious and even sinister figure. Who was he, anyway? What was he after? Further complications arose, when on the very night the 'Kherson landowner'— unable to sleep after the ball—kept cursing at his inn Nozdryov and all his ancestors, a strange equipage, resembling a 'full-cheeked rounded melon on wheels,' creaked and rumbled through the deserted streets of the town. The melon was 'full of cotton cushions in the shape of pouches, rolling-pins and simple pillows, stuffed with racks of bread, fancy loaves, doughnuts and pasties, and bread-rings made of boiled dough. Chicken pies and salt-fish pies peeped out at the top.' Amidst all this culinary profusion there sat the old widow Korobochka, who came hurrying to the town in order to make enquiries about the prices for dead souls: the mere suspicion that Chichikov might have cheated her out of a few roubles had made her frantic. So her arrival helped to fan the smouldering rumours into a fire. And what a fire! Soon the whole town set its tongues wagging and whispering about Chichikov's dark doings. Even people who had not been lured out of their rooms for years now joined the chorus of general condemnation of the man whom only a few days earlier everybody had looked up to as a model of decency, of social and moral perfection. In the meantime the hero himself, who had contracted a cold, was confined to his bed, with a bag full of camomile and camphor on his swollen cheeks, and had not the remotest idea of the hostility rising against him. One of the rumours would even have it that there was a secret liaison between Chichikov and the Governor's daughter. Detailed accounts of how Chichikov, helped by Nozdryov, had made all the arrangements for eloping with her were afloat. According to some good souls, Chichikov first had an illicit love-affair with the girl's mother, and only after that made a proposal to her daughter. But as the jilted mother would not hear of such an impious union, Chichikov bravely decided to elope with the lady of his heart.

No flights of fancy were now daring enough for those engaged in tarnishing Chichikov's name. Some of his former admirers maintained that he was a maker of counterfeit notes; others, that he was a robber-chief in disguise, or perhaps even Napoleon himself, who had escaped from his island prison and was now wandering over Holy Russia in order to bring about her ruin. Most perturbed were, however, the local officials. One of them, the thick-browed prosecutor, was so affected by all the rumours, each more puzzling than the last, that he

fell to brooding, and suddenly, for no rhyme or reason, as the saying is, died. Whether it was a paralytic stroke or some other attack, while he was sitting at the table, he, at any rate, flopped forward on his face. As is usual on such occasions, people cried out 'Good God!' and flinging up their hands sent for the doctor to bleed him, but they saw that the prosecutor was a soulless corpse. It was only then that they recognized with regret that he had really had a soul, though he had always been too modest to show it.

On his recovery, Chichikov (spick and span, warmly wrapped up, and sprinkled with eau de Cologne) set out again on his visits. To his astonishment people were either not 'at home' or else received him with undisguised dismay. Nozdryov alone did not mind his company. In fact, it was he who called on Chichikov. Having reported to him with relish all the scandal, he ended by asking the 'Kherson landowner' for a loan of three thousand roubles. But by this time Chichikov had put two and two together, and decided to move on. Which he did on the following day. As it happened, his carriage was held up for a few minutes by the prosecutor's funeral. While looking from behind the curtain of his chaise at the procession of bareheaded officials and at the mourning caps of the ladies, Chichikov fell to elegiac musing of his own:

'So much for the prosecutor. He lived and lived and then died! And now they will print in the newspapers that he passed away to the grief of his subordinates and of all humanity, an honoured citizen, a devoted father, a faithful husband, and they will write all sorts of nonsense; they will very likely add that he was followed to the grave by the lamentations of widows and orphans; and yet if one goes into the facts of the case, it turns out on investigation that there was nothing special about you but your thick eyebrows, . . . Well, it is a good thing we met the funeral; they say meeting a funeral means good luck.'

At the beginning of the novel Chichikov had emerged, so to speak, from nowhere. Now, at the end of it, he disappears into the same nebulous nowhere, leaving in the reader—for all the amusing descriptions—a feeling of vague metaphysical tedium. It was through Chichikov, as well as through the background he moved in (the background of the serf-owning and bureaucratic strata), that Gogol paraded all brands of philistinism as anti-life, subhuman in its very essence. The pathos of the book, whatever its purport, was again ethical rather than social: the pathos of a man who exposed the stifling vacuum of mere 'existers' mainly in order to reject it. And in this he succeeded.

5

Chichikov's departure, preceded by a history of his chequered former career, concludes the first volume of *Dead Souls*. Gogol began a second volume in December 1843, but only the drafts of the initial four chapters and the unfinished final chapter were found among his note-books. It is known, though, that several other chapters of the second volume were burned by him: one version in July 1845, and one shortly before his death in 1852. According to V. Kallash's investigations (recently endorsed by V. Gippius) the four chapters preserved are part of the version Gogol wrote after 1845, and which he may or may not have completed. The draft of the last chapter, however, is thought to be a remnant of the version he burned in 1845. To all intents and purposes, the second volume was to repeat the pattern of the first, but on a higher and more 'positive' moral level. In his preface to the second edition of *Dead Souls* (1846) Gogol pointed out that, whereas the first volume had shown the defects of the Russian man, better people and better characters would appear in its continuation—a promise which he actually kept to some extent in the fragments of the second volume. This time we meet Chichikov, with his chaise and his two servants, in another part of Russia. He is still buying up 'dead souls' from various landowners whose portraits are memorable—as in the first volume—on account of their typified defects. Chichikov himself has become more enterprising, more adventurous if anything, and in the plot there is a promise of greater complications. There even were to be in it references to the Decembrist revolt of 1825. From the few preserved chapters one can conclude that Gogol's power in portraying negative characters had hardly diminished. He may not have felt the inspiration he had known while writing the first volume, but his descriptive talent and his psychological intuition were still there. And they remained with him at least as long as he abstained

from presenting to his readers ready-made paragons of virtue.
The indolent Tentetnikov is particularly well portrayed, and
Tentetnikov's experiences in civil service may reflect those of
Gogol during his early Petersburg days. Then there are the
'superfluous' gentleman Platonov, the childishly self-important
General Betrishchev, the crazy Koshkaryov, the hospitable glut-
ton Pyetukh, the seedy Khlobuyev—all of them impressive
enough even in their sketchy state.

No one, however, will be able to say the same thing about
such a 'positive' and respectable specimen as the kulak Kostanzhoglo in the third and fourth chapters, or the philanthropic
merchant Murazov in the mangled final chapter. In Kostanzhoglo one feels at least plenty of guts; but as for Murazov,
he is just a shadow who cannot open his mouth without uttering
some moral platitudes fit for a schoolboy's primer. Chichikov is,
of course, so much impressed by Kostanzhoglo that he decides
there and then to become a landowner of the same lofty
kind. With which laudable aim he buys (rather profitably)
Khlobuyev's ruined estate.

> He felt delighted; delighted because he had now become
> a landowner, an owner not of an imaginary but of a real
> estate with land and all appurtenances and serfs—serfs
> not creatures of a dream, existing only in imagination, but
> real and substantial. And at last he began prancing up and
> down and rubbing his hands, and humming and murmur-
> ing, and putting his fist to his mouth blew a march on it as
> on a trumpet, and even uttered aloud a few encouraging
> words and nicknames addressed to himself, such as 'bull-
> dog' and 'little cockerel.'

Unfortunately, in his eagerness to get rich quick he fakes the
will of the same Khlobuyev's wealthy aunt, and is landed in
prison. Here the God-fearing Murazov comes to see him and,
after a long homily, promises to do all he can to get him out
of the place. Chichikov himself, who has not yet been deprived
of his worldly wisdom, gives a huge bribe to be distributed
among the officials in charge of the case. In consequence of this

operation (joined to Murazov's virtue), Chichikov is released, but with the proviso that he shall leave the district at once. Evicted in this manner, he leaves the town as at the end of the first volume, but this time he does it with a vague promise of moral regeneration. His soul has by now reached a stage in which it can be likened to a 'building that has been pulled down to be rebuilt into a new one, while the new one has not yet been begun, because no definite plan has come as yet from the architect and the workers are in suspense.'

The 'architect' Gogol, who was passing at the time through an inner crisis of his own, had a plan according to which a third volume was to be added—presumably in order to turn the whole of *Dead Souls* into a Russian counterpart of Dante's *Divine Comedy*, but in prose. If the first volume, with the low level of human consciousness shown in it, reflected the *Inferno* of the Russian soul, the planned second and third volumes were to be its *Purgatory* and *Paradise* respectively. To crown it all, the regenerated Chichikov was to be saved in the end (most likely in the shape of a patriarchal God-fearing serf-owner enjoying with a good conscience the proceeds of his former swindling). There even was an 'ideal' Governor, waiting to join this league of perfection. But here, too, as in real life, perfection looks too good to be true. It is stilted and hollow. All things considered, a continuation of *Dead Souls* was hardly necessary; and least of all in this spirit, since the finished volume is complete as it stands.

This does not mean that it is without flaws. Its somewhat loose structure is one of them. The finale of the novel is slowed down and actually weakened by the interpolation of Chichikov's biography. It is true that without such a picture of Chichikov's past *Dead Souls* would have lost much of its psychological motivation. On the other hand, it might as well have been given earlier. Then, there are Gogol's frequent digressions, personal comments, lyrical and moralizing passages, many of which seem to have been squeezed in when the 'epic' had already been finished. This is why their tone and mood differ from the general atmosphere of the book: as though they had been written by another person. Gogol actually ends his masterpiece with a paean to his own country, which he compares with a swift *troika* recklessly flying into the unknown distance.

> Russia, whither fliest thou? Answer! She gives no answer. The ringing of the bells melts into music; the air, torn to shreds, whirs and rushes like the wind, everything there is on earth is flying by, and the other nations, with looks askance, make way for her and draw aside.

What one wonders at in the end is Gogol's own inconsistency. How was it possible to show throughout the whole of the novel one gloomy picture of Russia after another, one knave after another, and then burst into a paean almost suggestive of a Russian equivalent of *Deutschland über alles*! But such was Gogol. A bundle of contradictions in his character and also in his art. There are plenty of them in *Dead Souls*. Still, they are redeemed by the excellence of the novel as a whole.

6

Dead Souls represented the high-water mark of Gogol's art. But its reception, not unlike that of *The Revizor*, was a mixture of enthusiasm and vituperation. Constantine Aksakov was not afraid to compare Gogol's epic power with that of Homer, while Faddei Bulgarin and his clique were doing their best to persuade readers that Gogol was a slanderer of Russia and that his talent did not rise above the level of Paul de Kock. On the other hand, the novel found an ardent admirer in Belinsky, who wrote a series of articles about it and stressed, apart from its artistic merits, also its social significance. Gogol, of course, never made a direct attack either on serfdom or on autocracy. Indirectly, however, *Dead Souls* contained enough powder or even dynamite to undermine these two institutions—simply by showing their baleful effect on man and life. The impression the novel had made upon the younger generation is testified to by no less a person than Alexander Herzen. This is what he says on the subject in his French pamphlet, *Du*

Développement des Idées Révolutionnaires en Russie (1851), when talking about Gogol the writer: 'Having made the transition from his Ukrainians and Cossacks to the Russian proper, Gogol leaves people aside in order to tackle his two most ruthless enemies: the official and the squire. No one before him has made such a complete investigation of the pathologic anatomy of the Russian *chinovnik* [official]. With a smile on his lips he penetrates into the most hidden folds of that filthy and wicked soul. . . . *Dead Souls* shook the whole of Russia. It is a picture of her disease, painted by a master's hand. Gogol's art is like a cry of shame and terror on the part of a man who has been degraded by the vulgarity of existence and has suddenly perceived in a mirror his animal-like features. But in order to release such a cry from one's breast, one must possess some healthy portions of body as well, and a great capacity for restoring one's health.'

Nor did it take long before translations of the novel began to appear abroad. Its first German version (by Philip Loebenstein) was published as early as 1846. Together with a volume of his translated stories—*Russische Novellen*—it launched Gogol's literary fame in Central Europe. In France, Gogol's works became known in 1845, when Louis Viardot, helped by Ivan Turgenev, issued a volume of his narratives: *Taras Bulba, A Madman's Diary, The Coach, The Old-World Landowners,* and *Viy.* The critic Sainte-Beuve, who had met Gogol in 1838, wrote an enthusiastic review of this book in the December number of *La Revue des Deux Mondes,* 1845. In 1851, the same periodical published Mérimée's appreciative essay on Gogol. Yet *Dead Souls* had to wait until 1859 before appearing in French in two almost simultaneous versions: one by Ernest Charrière (a former tutor to Count Sollogub's family) and the other by Eugène Moreau. It is a pity that Charrière was misled into translating also an absurdly unreadable 'continuation' of the second volume, concocted (in 1857) by an obscure literary jobber, Vashchenko-Zakharchenko, whose production appears, alas! in an English translation as well.

In England *Dead Souls* started out on a somewhat peculiar

adventure in 1854, when, at the height of the Crimean campaign, it was published anonymously under the title *Home Life in Russia*. In order to make its contents look the more authentic as a mirror of Russia, a suitable preface informed the readers about its origin. 'The Work is written,' so it says, 'by a Russian nobleman, who offered the MS. in English to the publishers, and the Editor's task has been confined to altering such verbal errors as might be expected, when we bear in mind that the Author has written in a language which is not his own. The story may be said to be unique. It gives us an insight into the internal circumstances and relations of Russian society, which only a Russian could afford us. The Nosdrieffs [Nozdryovs] are an exceptional class, whose type is peculiar to a half-civilization where a blow is accounted as no disgrace and "giving the lie" imparts no stigma. And yet men who quietly pocket such insults, we find, are tolerated in good society, and strange to say, are not thought the worse of on that account. The Napoleonic dictum, *"grattez le Russe, et vous trouverez le Tartare,"* is in this instance most fully verified.' After some further comments in the same vein, the 'Editor' apologizes in the name of the author (Gogol had died more than two years before) in the following unperturbed manner: 'In conclusion, we may regret that we are not at liberty to mention the author's name—not that the work requires any further verification, for its genuineness is avouched by almost every line—but the truth is, that the writer is still anxious to return to his native country, and is perfectly well aware that the avowal of his handiwork, and such a display of his satirical powers, will not serve as a special recommendation, except, possibly, as a passport to the innermost regions of the Siberian wilds.' In addition, the finale of the 'edited' novel is also a triumph of justice. When Chichikov hastily leaves the town, he is followed by the Commissioner of Police and another gentleman on horseback. One of them hands over to him a document, on perusing which Chichikov turns as pale as death. 'The imperial messenger then pointed to a sinister-looking carriage, called a Siberian kibitka, into which our hero was assisted, without being able to utter a syllable, and the next moment he was a dead man.'

Many translations of Gogol's novel have since appeared and are still appearing in Europe, America, and all over the world. The passage of time, far from impairing its reputation, has only enhanced it. *Dead Souls* now ranks as a Russian classic. It is also one of the literary masterpieces of the world. And there is no reason why the verdict of the future should be different.

Chapter 8

The Moralist Versus the Artist

1

WITH THE publication of *Dead Souls*, Gogol's literary activities (as far as their creative side was concerned) were practically finished. But while the artist in him was receding, Gogol the moralist began to assert himself, and for a number of reasons. After Pushkin's tragic death in 1837 the leadership in Russian letters had naturally passed to Gogol, who was now more and more inclined to interpret it in a spiritual and moral sense. What his country needed was not 'amusing' or even frivolous literature, but that inner guidance which he was called upon by Providence itself to give. Was not the whole of Russia waiting for vivifying, prophetic words which would 'burn the hearts of men.'[28] And since God had endowed him with the gift of word, was it not his duty to use it in precisely this sense? In the last chapter of *Dead Souls* he actually interpolated a lyrical passage ending with the question: 'Russia! what wouldst thou of me? What is the mysterious bond between us? Why dost thou gaze at me thus, and why is everything within thee turning upon me eyes full of expectation?'

But Gogol thought he knew by now what she wanted. He only doubted, now and then, whether he was fully entitled to the mission he had been chosen for. Aware of his own sins and weaknesses, he could not but vacillate at times. But the doubts only spurred on his own moral endeavours towards the kind of perfection he needed in order to become worthy of all that God and Providence wanted him to accomplish in this world. Trusting the divine Grace, he wrote to Zhukovsky from Berlin on 26th June 1842, while still flushed with the success of his novel: 'In my heart there lives a profound and irrefutable faith that heavenly power will help me to climb that ladder which I must climb, although I am still on its lowest rungs. There is a long way to go yet; a long process of spiritual education lies in front of me. My soul must become cleaner than the mountain snow and brighter than the skies; only then shall I feel strong enough for my great task; only then will the mystery of my life be solved.'

Gogol's aspirations of this kind were most sincere, but they contained a few disturbing elements. His archaic idea of a direct personal contact and personal transactions with the divine Power watching all his steps (the ladder he was to climb included) was one of them. There even was a second and more dangerous one: the unconscious moral pride, almost inseparable from his role of one 'elect.' Since he was put so high above other mortals in order to exhort and guide them, it was from now on his duty not only to use his gift of word, but also to show by personal example the path to virtue. To be *only* an artist was no longer enough. His task now obliged him to impart to his own life, as well as to his future writings (above all to the projected continuation of *Dead Souls*), a moral and 'religious' purpose. Thus he hoped to foster the victory of good over evil for the benefit of thousands of people. Such, at any rate, was God's will—working through Gogol.

2

It is fair to say that an attitude of this nature was conditioned by Gogol's early upbringing and by his general cast of mind. It may have been further stimulated by some of his Roman experiences—those in particular which kept stirring his peculiar ambitions and inclinations. In Rome he was a frequent guest of the talented Princess Zinaida Volkonskaya, a Russian convert to Catholicism.[29] It was in Rome, too, that he met some of those Polish dreamers (mostly refugees) who were fond of mixing pseudo-mystical fantasies with pseudo-political activities. A deep impression was there made upon him also by the death of the youthful Count Joseph Vielgorsky (in 1839), perhaps the only person towards whom—judging by his lyrical fragment, *Nights at the Villa*—Gogol ever felt something like unreserved friendship. In addition he was closely associated with the Russian religious painter Alexander A. Ivanov, who was living in Rome at the same time as Friedrich Johann Overbeck, the head of the religious Nazarenes group of German artists.

So much for Rome. When, in 1842, Gogol was overwhelmed by the reception of *Dead Souls* in Russia, he saw in all that only another sign of that dispensation which divine Providence had reserved for him. So he was the more anxious to be morally worthy of it. For this purpose he even conceived the idea of going on a pilgrimage to Jerusalem, where he hoped miraculously to shed the old Adam and grow as perfect as God wanted him to be. He had to postpone this journey for several years. Which did not prevent him, though, from advertising it among his friends and even writing openly about it at the time he was planning and writing the second volume of *Dead Souls*. 'Who can say,' he asked Sergei Aksakov in a letter (on 18th August 1842), 'that there is not a mysterious bond between this work of mine and my distant journey? And who knows whether there is not, perhaps, a profound and miraculous bond between all this and the whole of my life, the whole of my future, although no one else may be aware of it? So all respect to Providence. This I say from the very depth of my soul. Remember: when the world is at its pettiest and life has become emptier than ever; when everything is covered with egoism and coldness and no one believes in miracles—it is precisely at such a time that the miracle of miracles can take place . . . in the same way as the greatest sea-storm arises when the surface of the sea is quieter than usual. My soul senses the coming bliss and knows that our efforts to attain it are enough to make it descend, by God's all-highest Grace, into our hearts.' After which there followed a homily simply as a matter of his prophetic routine: 'And so let your thoughts grow every day brighter and brighter; let your faith in God be unshakable, and beware of being saddened by anything that men stupidly call misfortune.'

Gogol was obviously in one of his periodic fits of elation.

Having lulled himself into the proud belief of being a vehicle of God's will, he was convinced that all that was happening to him had a deep religious and moral import. When in 1845 he had fallen very ill at Frankfurt and then as though by a miracle suddenly recovered, he ascribed his recovery to the same divine Will. So he was the more eager to put his art into God's service and thus promote the victory of the moral principle here on earth. Looking back on his past achievements, he now tried to interpret them—*retrospectively*—as a camouflaged process of his own moral purification through art and through laughter. In *The Denouement of The Revizor* (1846), for example, he exhorted his readers not to forget the kind of laughter 'our lower passions are afraid of. . . . In the same manner as we laugh at the vices in other people, let us magnanimously laugh at all the vices we find in ourselves.' In a more personal confession he completed this advice by saying that all the readers who laughed at his characters were actually laughing at him, since these were a projection of his own nastiness. His artistic creation was thus declared as having been definitely a kind of catharsis. 'Taking some bad feature of mine, I presented it under a different name and in a different role, trying to make it appear in my eyes as a deadly enemy—an enemy who had inflicted a terrible injury upon me; so I persecuted it with irony and malice, with anything I could lay my hands on. . . . I have already freed myself from several nasty features by projecting them into my characters, by laughing at them and making other people laugh at them.' In *The Denouement of The Revizor* Gogol tried to interpret even his great comedy in the light of a moral and 'mystical' allegory. The God-forsaken provincial hole, ruled over by the *gorodnichy*, he now proclaimed to be the city of the soul; the corrupt officials were our passions; the windbag Khlestakov represented our 'worldly conscience,' whereas the Government Inspector in the last scene of the last act was the 'true conscience' each of us will have to face after death. All this is rank nonsense, but highly indicative of Gogol's state of mind at the time he was engaged in writing the second volume of *Dead Souls*.

3

It did not take long, however, before some alarming factors began to creep in. Gogol was doing all he could to brace himself for his 'great task' and to justify all that Providence expected of him, when he noticed that precisely when he was most anxious to give his edifying moral heroes flesh and blood, the inspiration he had once known was on the wane. His talent was still there, but the 'invisible hand' which formerly had guided his pen seemed to have grown sluggish or even intent on withdrawing altogether. Gogol, who had created such intense negative characters by projecting into them his own 'nastiness,' could not but come to the conclusion that the only way of creating convincing 'positive' heroes was to project into them his own virtues. But in order to do this, he himself had to become as virtuous as possible. He made brave efforts in this direction, but without much avail. His process of writing remained slow. In spite of his endeavours, his moral characters just would not take shape. Besides, his own artistic conscience wanted to be satisfied with the results of such moral aspirations, and this was not easy. As he could not blend the two in a satisfactory manner, he was at cross-purposes with himself to the extent of burning the first version of the second volume of *Dead Souls* during his illness in 1845. Less than two years later he wrote apropos of this literary *auto-da-fé*: 'I thank God that he gave me enough strength to do it. As soon as the flames had gutted the last sheets of my book, its contents returned to my mind in a purified shape like a phoenix arisen from the ashes, and I suddenly perceived the chaotic state of what I had deemed to be full of order and harmony. The publication of the second volume, such as it was, would have done more harm than good. . . . One should not talk about things lofty and beautiful without showing there and then the path leading up to them and accessible to all. This feature, which should have been my primary consideration, was badly developed in the second volume of my *Dead Souls*, and so it had to be burned.'

But despite the 'purified shape' arisen from the ashes of the gutted manuscript, the moralist in Gogol continued to fare as badly as before. His pen refused to draw the paragons of virtue his countrymen were in need of in order to save their own souls. Did this mean that divine Providence was actually growing reluctant to use Gogol for her designs? The mere suspicion of this kind was enough to make him increase his efforts towards personal perfection and thus become worthy of what he regarded as his message and his great life-task. In fact, he was now so impatient to pour out the message he had to convey, that in the end he decided to do it independently of his art, in plain sermons and admonitions. So he embarked on preparing a whole volume of these, during which process he worked himself into the appropriae state of mind and began dispensing wisdom like an oracle. The adulation of his countrymen both at home and abroad only spurred on his 'Messiah complex' and, together with it, that self-assertive spiritual pride of his which strikes one so unpleasantly in his letters. The blame is not entirely on his side. Much of it rests on those Russian friends of his who from the outset did all they could to make him see himself and his doings in the wrong perspective. His principal friend in Russia, Madame Rosset-Smirnova (a former lady-in-waiting who became something of a repentant Magdalen), was suffering from fits of pietism, and these tallied well with the moods of Gogol, whose platonic attachment to her still remains something of a puzzle. He was also surrounded by a bevy of devout society-ladies, most of whom had long passed their prime and were therefore glad to listen to Gogol the 'Teacher,' even while regarding him as their social inferior. (There were, however, a few genuine Christian souls among them: Madame Khomyakova,[30] for instance, or the warm-hearted but muddle-headed old Countess Nadya Sheremetyeva). Finally, the Slavophils and their camp-followers, who fawned on Gogol, actually made him their *enfant gâté*: partly because they saw in him an ally and a potential exponent of their own conservative ideas. The writer Ivan T. Panayev,[31] who was present at a dinner-party in Gogol's honour, describes him as a man who 'could not but be aware of all this worship and adulation, and accepted it as something due to him even when he tried to veil his satisfaction by a seeming indifference. There was something strained and artificial in his behaviour, something which painfully impressed all those who wanted to see in him a human being rather than a genius.'

Gogol could not resist such flattering proofs of his importance at a time when he was so desperately trying to ward off misgivings with regard to his mission. He continued to insist upon his great task in his private thoughts and private letters, until his would-be prophetic moods became redolent of a spiritual Khlestakov. What could have been more presuming than the way in which he demanded of his friends and acquaintances that they should listen to him with pious reverence! Some of his letters of that period are quite incredible, however interesting they may be psychologically. To Pogodin, for instance, he wrote from Rome: 'I am homeless, I am beaten and lulled by the waves, but I lean only upon that anchor of pride which the higher powers have bestowed upon me. . . . You must cherish me not because of myself—no, but because in this vessel is enclosed a treasure.' Incidentally, when the same friend's wife died, Gogol did not mind consoling the bereaved widower, who was frantic with grief, with the promise that from now on he [Pogodin] would be helped by Jesus Christ to become a gentleman 'which you are neither by education nor by inclination!' To this he added the tactful remark: 'She [i.e. Pogodin's deceased wife] speaks through me.'

Fits of spiritual Khlestakovism were accompanied in him by piety and even by acts of ostentatious philanthropy. In his preface to a new edition of *The Revizor* (in 1846) Gogol not only announced that the proceeds would be given to the poor, but appointed a special committee of society-ladies, mentioned by name, who would collect the money and dispose of it according to his wishes. In the meantime his own financial affairs were in a chronic muddle and had to be disentangled, again and again, by his friends, notably by Aksakov and Shevyryov, from whom he borrowed whenever he could.

4

To see in all these contortions only a pose would be unfair. His personality was much too complex for such simple solutions and, besides, there was a tragic side to it. No matter how unpleasant some of his features may have been, there was always a layer of genuine idealism and of moral nostalgia behind them. Sincerity and pretence, conceit and humility, Khlestakovism and a truly severe attitude towards himself were so strongly intertwined in him that it was often impossible to tell one from the other. Yet those friends of his who admired in him the artist that he was, or had been, could not help resenting the defects they saw in Gogol the man. An example is the candid letter Sergei Aksakov addressed to him as a friendly if severe warning on 9th December 1846.

'For a long time I have felt dissatisfied with the trend of your religious outlook,' he wrote. 'Not that I, being a bad Christian, understood it badly and in consequence feared it, but because your Christian humility struck me as spiritual pride. Many passages in your letters troubled me; but they were expressed with such poetic brilliance, with such sincerity of feeling, that I dared not obey my inner voice, which condemned them. So I tried to interpret my unpleasant impressions in a sense favourable to you. . . . Meanwhile your new outlook kept developing and growing. My fears reappeared with greater force: every letter I received from you confirmed them. Instead of your one-time friendly and warm-hearted utterances, they contained the sermons of a preacher, sermons which were obscure, sometimes prophesying but always cold and—worst of all—full of conceit in the ragged garb of humility. I could prove this by many an extract, but I think it superfluous and, besides, it would be too painful for me. Next, you sent us, together with a puzzling letter, the soul-saving book of Thomas à Kempis and detailed prescriptions as to how, when and to what extent we ought to use it; you also promised they would make a radical change in our spiritual life. . . . My apprehension turned into downright fear, and I sent you a frank, sharp letter. At that time a terrible misfortune was impending over me: I was irretrievably losing the sight of one eye and had begun to feel that the other eye, too, was getting weaker. Overcome with despair, I poured out my grief to you, but received in answer a few dry, cold lines which, far from consoling the heart of an afflicted friend, only pained it.[32] Then you yourself fell ill for a long time;[33] soon after your slow recovery my agonizing pain began and it still continues. There are not many things in which my heart takes a deep interest; but it has always been interested in you in the first place. Your physical health is now evidently better, and your activities have started afresh; but what activities! Each of your deeds has been a blow to me, and each one stronger than the last.'

Here follow certain accusations, of which I will quote only the one referring to Gogol's philanthropy. 'My friend,' Aksakov asks, 'where is that Christian humility which bids us do good so that the left hand should not know what the right hand is doing? You are now forming, openly and so that the whole of Russia should hear of it, a Beneficent Society of your own: you are nominating its members and giving them instructions with regard to activities which cannot be carried out, and which are in any case quite incompatible with the ideas of decency. How can you imagine that the persons appointed by you, for the most part ladies, will be so indiscriminate and so immodest as publicly to accept the role of benefactresses you have conferred upon them! . . . Where is your formerly clear, sane idea of publicity and ostentation in matters of beneficence? . . . You have forgotten all about human modesty.'

Surely an ominous warning. But it came too late. For by that time Gogol was in high fettle. Aware of Russia's 'eyes full of expectation' resting on him, he was determined to come up to scratch and to prove that he really had something to say for the sake of her spiritual and moral salvation—even if he had to do it outside that artistic form which until then had been his principal medium. So he gathered together all his wisdom and published it in *Selected Passages from Correspondence with my Friends*. It was the fate of this book that brought his inner and external crisis to a head.

Chapter 9

The Defeat

1

THE UNPRETENTIOUS though long-winded title of *Selected Passages from Correspondence with my Friends* was a misnomer. For in spite of Gogol's assertion to the contrary the book had little to do with his actual letters. Secondly, the ideas and opinions voiced in it were addressed not so much to his friends as to the entire nation. So it was more like a collection of thirty-two didactic essays, exhortations and sermons (with three of them deleted) in epistolary form and in a tone which excluded beforehand any objections to the wisdom enounced. This time, if ever, Gogol spoke *ex cathedra*, or rather from his own private pulpit. The solemnity of his tone and manner testified to the seriousness with which he must have pieced these 'letters' together. And he was so sure that this latest work would stagger his country like a new Revelation that, shortly before it was published, he wrote to Pletnyov from Schwalbach (on 30th August 1846): 'Here at last is my request! As a faithful friend you must fulfil this friendly request of mine. Give up all your occupations and get busy with the printing of *Selected Passages from Correspondence with my Friends*. This book is needed by all; I can say no more at present. The rest will be explained to you by the book itself. It will make everything clear to you even before it is printed, and all the doubts you suffer from will forthwith disappear.' In the spring of 1846 P. V. Annenkov met Gogol in Bamberg, and during their talk in the cathedral Gogol invited him to spend the winter of the same year in Naples where he himself intended to stay. 'You will hear in Naples things which you do not expect,' he promised. 'There I will tell you things which are of importance to you . . . to you personally. . . . No man can foresee where the much needed help is waiting for him. . . . I tell you, come to Naples. . . . There I will disclose a secret for which you will be grateful. . . . No one can tell where he will find a new life.'

The 'secret' was of course the contents of the book he was then feverishly preparing for publication and which duly came out on New Year's Day 1847, or, to be exact, the day before. But the reception it met with was enough to cool down Gogol's prophetic ardour once and for all. Neither his unpleasantly high-pitched voice nor the aplomb with which he enounced his high-falutin' platitudes was likely to appeal to those he had in mind. Intelligent readers could not but feel that here Gogol was holding forth about Church and Christianity, Russia and the West, marriage and family, education, literature, theatre, priests, landowners, Governors, and even Governors' wives, regardless of whether or not he was competent to have any say in such matters. The Pecksniffian tone of the Preface was enough to put one off, let alone its unconscious spiritual exhibitionism.

'I was gravely ill; death was already near. Having gathered the remnants of my strength and taken advantage of the complete clarity of my mind, I wrote a Testament in which, among other things, I put on my friends the obligation to publish after my death some of my letters. I was anxious to redeem at least in this manner the uselessness of everything I have published until now, since in my letters, in the opinion of those to whom they were written, there is more substance needed by a man than in my [literary] works. Divine Grace warded off the hand of death. I have nearly recovered; my state of health is better. But I feel how weak my strength is and how I am reminded every day that my life still hangs on a thread. While preparing, moreover, for a distant journey to the Holy Land—a journey during which anything may happen, I wanted to let my countrymen have a parting gift from me. Having succeeded in collecting my recent letters, I have chosen from them all the passages concerning the

problems which are at present of interest to our society.
... Finally I have also added my Testament, so that in
case of my death it could be immediately endorsed by law,
with all my readers as witnesses.'

Further on, Gogol insists that never before has he experienced
such a strong desire to be useful and that this is his chance of
offering help. Of course, 'it is not we who help, but God who
imparts power to words otherwise devoid of it.' He humbly
asks each of his readers not only to read *Selected Passages*
several times, but to buy right away several copies of the book
and distribute them among those who are unable to buy it. He
also implores his friends and foes to forgive him in case his
former works, or his personal behaviour, should have offended
them. In the end he promises his countrymen to pray for all of
them in Jerusalem, at our Saviour's tomb, provided again that
divine Grace does not turn away from his prayers.

It would perhaps be unfair to condemn his book wholesale.
Some of his observations—those concerning the theatre, or such
Russian poets as Derzhavin, Yazykov, Zhukovsky, and of
course Pushkin—may be sound enough. He even gives in it
some intriguing observations with regard to *Dead Souls*. Yet the
prevalent mood, which crops up time and again, is one of
reactionary Utopia with a theocratic flavour. Particularly irri-
tating is the way in which Gogol tries to solve important social
and political problems at one stroke, so to speak, with the air
of a man who is still rooted in the 'patriarchal' mentality of
serfdom and sees in the Russian autocracy a divine form of
government. Here Gogol actually fawned on the very system
he had once—hardly more than ten years earlier—attacked in
The Revizor. God himself was now given the status of a patriarchal heavenly landowner. And since His decree was that
things should remain as He had created them, any revolt against
the powers that be, against autocracy, oppression and serfdom,
would be contrary to His divine will and wisdom.

As an example of Gogol's homilies this advice in *The Letter
to a Landowner* may be quoted: 'Your remarks concerning

schools are quite to the point. To give a peasant school-educa-
tion in order to enable him to read the shallow pamphlets published by our European humanitarians is sheer nonsense.' In
the same letter he pointed out that 'in a village where Christ's
faith rules, the peasants have shovelfuls of money.' Equally
enlightened were his views on a number of other subjects. He,
moreover, advocated personal persuasion as the best method
for spreading his truths.[34] Being a Christian, Gogol the teacher
and preacher was of course anxious to make his smugness
appear as modest as possible. Hence his self-accusations. In his
excess of modesty he even went so far as to entreat his fellow-
citizens not to fall into despair nor to erect a statue to him,
once he was dead.

2

The general reaction to such a book could have been fore-
seen. The shock is produced among liberal-minded intellectuals,
and even among Gogol's friends in the conservative Slavophil
camp, was quite unbelievable. Whereas the progressive 'West-
erners' saw in him an open advocate of autocracy, the more
religious Slavophils found it difficult to forgive the spiritual
pride permeating the pages of his new work. The Government
alone greeted *Selected Passages* with a crooning voice of ap-
proval—partly because it was taken for granted that Gogol had
written it with ulterior motives. There were rumours that he
had hoped thereby to ingratiate himself with the heir apparent
(the subsequent Tsar Alexander II) and be appointed tutor to
his son. Sergei Aksakov was so nonplussed that he sent on
27th January 1847 a severe letter to Gogol in which he said:
'You have entirely lost your way, you blunder about, you con-
tradict yourself all the time, and while thinking that you serve
heaven and humanity you offend both God and man.' And less
than two weeks later (on 8th February 1847) he wrote to his
son Ivan: 'Gogol does not cease to occupy my thoughts from
morning till night; he has really gone mad—there can be no
doubt about it; but—I must confess—there is plenty of rascality

and cunning in his madness. In their own fashion, madmen too are rogues and cheats: and their madness awakens in me both pity and loathing.'

Blows continued to shower upon Gogol from right and left. The worst of them all came, however, from his former champion and admirer, Belinsky. As it happened, Belinsky first wrote a long review of the book in the second number of *The Contemporary*, 1847. It was a frank yet on the whole reserved criticism, warning Gogol the artist against Gogol the 'prophet.' In June of the same year Gogol sent an answer to his critic, who at the time was undergoing a cure at the Austrian spa, Salzbrunn. It was to this answer that Belinsky replied, on 15th July 1847, with his famous letter—the most indignant and passionate letter in Russian literature. In view of the influence it had on the moral and political consciousness of the Russian intelligentsia, one will perhaps be excused for quoting at least a few extracts.

'One can bear the feeling of wounded pride,' fumed Belinsky, 'but it is impossible to bear the feeling of outraged truth, of outraged humanity. It is impossible to be silent when, under the cloak of religion and the protection of the knout, lies and immorality are preached as truth and virtue. And you say that your book could only have been written as the result of a painful inner process and of spiritual illumination from on high! Either you are a sick man—and you must quickly submit to a curse, or else. . . . I dare not utter my thought! . . . You preacher of the knout, apostle of ignorance, defender of obscurantism and darkest oppression; you eulogist of Tartar manners—what are you doing! Look under your feet—you stand over an abyss. . . . I can well understand why you base your doctrine on the Orthodox Church: she has always been a supporter of the knout and a flatterer of despotism; but why should you mix up Christ with all this? What have you found in common between Him and any Church, especially the Orthodox Church? He was the first to announce to men the doctrine of freedom, equality and brotherhood, and it was with His own martyrdom that He sealed the sincerity of His teaching, which remained a salvation for men only until the time when it became organized into a Church and based on dogmas. And the Church herself became hierarchic, that is, a defender of inequality, a flatterer of power, an enemy of brotherhood among men—which she still is in our days. . . . As for the humility which you preach, in the first place it is not new, and secondly it savours of fearful conceit on the one hand, and of a shameful abasement of your own human dignity on the other. The idea of becoming a paragon of abstract perfection, and of rising above your fellow-men through humility, can only come from conceit or idiocy, and in either case leads to hypocrisy, cant and stagnation. You, moreover, took the liberty of cynically slandering in your book not only others (which is uncivil), but also your own person, which is disgusting; for if a man who strikes his fellow-beings in the face arouses indignation, a man striking his own face arouses contempt. No, you are only bemused and not enlightened; you have understood neither the form nor the spirit of contemporary Christianity. It is not the truth of Christ's doctrine that your book breathes, but the fear of death, hell and the devil.'[35]

3

Such criticism, and by the leading Russian critic, too, was more than Gogol could bear. It was like a *coup de grâce* which made him tumble from his 'prophetic' pinnacle into the slough of despond in the middle of which he capitulated with hardly any fight. Eventually he himself joined his attackers by adding to their blows a number of self-reproaches which he exaggerated with an almost masochistic pleasure. 'I displayed in my book so much of my own Khlestakov-like nature that I do not dare glance at it,' he wrote to Zhukovsky. 'How ashamed I am of myself, and how ashamed I feel before you, my good soul! I feel ashamed of having thought that I could be your equal. Truly, there is something of Khlestakov in me.'

But in spite of all he was still on the look-out for extenuating circumstances, however lame. One of these was to the effect that he had published *Selected Passages* not in order to teach others but to be taught by them—by their reactions to the book. He even tried to answer Belinsky's letter, but—judging by the fragments of his attempted reply—he was unable to summon sufficiently convincing arguments. There is, however, one passage among them which ought to be quoted on account of its pertinence. 'You say that Russia can only be saved by European civilization, but what a broad, limitless word you use! Had you at least defined what we should understand by civilization! There we see all sorts of *phalanstéres*, red and others—all of them ready to eat up one another; all of them full of such threatening and destructive ideas that every thinking head in Europe trembles and willy-nilly asks: Where is our civilization?' There are a few other thoughts one stumbles upon in this book —thoughts startling enough to make one see the tragic side of Gogol's character, despite his latent Khlestakovism. In his last 'Letter' (on the Russian Easter), for example, he gives vent to his *Weltgefuehl*, amidst all the modern speed, science and technique, in one cry of despair: 'Harder and harder is life. It grows more and more petty; and before the eyes of us all there rises the gigantic image of Tedium; it rises and keeps assuming infinite dimensions day in day out.'

But occasional utterances of this kind cannot make up for the defects of the book as a whole. Gogol realized this only when it was too late to do anything about it. He wrote *An Author's Confession*, which was above all an apology for his literary *faux pas*, but (like most apologies of this kind) fails to be convincing. The only time he came near the truth about *Selected Passages* was in the statement he made in his letter to Aksakov on 28th June 1847: 'Impatience made me publish my book. Seeing that I should not be able to master my *Dead Souls*, and genuinely grieving over the drabness of contemporary literature, I hastened to say a word or two about the vital problems I had wanted to embody and develop in living images and characters.'

4

In the conflict between his artistic and his moral conscience, Gogol eventually did his best to make the latter triumph even at the expense of his art. Yet, strange to say, the defeat brought upon him by *Selected Passages* was above all of a moral order. In this case, Gogol's literary fiasco was mild in comparison with those moral doubts and torments he was from now on forced to endure. What made things worse for him was the intense isolation he must have experienced while being hounded by friend and foe alike. At the same time he knew that in spite of all the 'Khlestakovism' of his book there was one thing in it his attackers had overlooked: his sincere wish to be sincere. In this state of moral and spiritual prostration, he was looking for support wherever he still hoped to find it, but in vain. Friends often treated him even worse than enemies. Gogol felt their lack of justice and did not mind saying so. It is enough to read the letter he sent to Sergei Aksakov from Frankfurt, on 10th June 1847, to see the weight of his bewilderment and his despair.

'For the sake of Christ Himself, put yourself in my place so as to get an idea of what I am passing through, and tell me: What am I to do? What and how am I now to write? If I had the power of saying a sincere word, my very tongue would remain tied. One can speak sincerely to those who have at least some faith in our sincerity; but if you deal with a man who has already formed his own opinion of you and sticks to it, then even the sincerest person will remain dumb, let alone me who (as you know) am reserved, and whose very reserve comes from my inability to explain myself. I beg you now, for the sake of Christ, not in the name of friendship but of that charity which is to be found in every good and compassionate soul—in the name of charity I beg you to put yourself in my position, because my heart is torn with grief, although I try to be brave and calm. My relations with those friends who were in a hurry to make friends with me before they had got to know me have now become too painful. I can hardly understand how it is I have not yet been driven mad. All I know is that my heart is broken, and that my will to action is paralyzed. A struggle with infuriated foes is always bearable, but God preserve us from the terrible battle with one's friends. Everything that is in us gets broken by it. My friend, I am broken—I cannot say more at present. But in so far as the constancy of my affection is concerned, I will only say that my heart is open to love more than ever. If I love and wish to love those who do not love me, how should I then fail to love those who do love me! But it is not love I beg of you, now. Instead of love, give me at least one drop of your pity, because—I repeat—my position is difficult. Put yourself in my place, and you will see that I suffer more than those whom I have offended. My friend, all I tell you is true.'

One step further, and we reach that last phase of Gogol's life in which he felt estranged not only from his former friends but from all the world; from God and man, and most of all from himself.

Chapter 10

The Last Act

1

AFTER THE FAILURE of *Selected Passages*, Gogol had some five more years to live—the unhappiest and inwardly most restless years he had known. Having seen God's will, as well as God's hand, at work in all the major happenings of his life, he was now logically compelled to see its interference also in the fiasco of his 'mission' and life-task. But why was he so cruelly punished? Was it because divine Providence had turned away from him on account of his conceit, his sins and his 'nastiness?' He knew he had not yet divested himself of them as completely as he had wished to. Hence his anxiety to make up for it all not only by exaggerated self-accusations but also by intensified ascetic practices. It was in such a mood that he resumed the second volume of *Dead Souls*. What he now decided to show in it (i.e. after the version burnt by him in 1845) were not so much paragons of virtue as characters who were on their path to virtue—the path he himself was in need of. Yet in spite of his resolve the inspiration continued to be absent. The process of writing was a pain for him. Gradually he became almost obsessed by the idea that God no longer needed his services. 'God, who knows better than I what time is suitable for our work, has withdrawn from me, for a long time, the capacity for literary creation,' he wrote to Madame Rosset-Smirovna. 'I tormented myself, I forced myself to write, I suffered heavily when I saw this helplessness of mine, and several times made myself ill through such forcing; yet I was not able to do anything, and all that came out of it was artificial and bad. Often, often was I overwhelmed by *ennui*, and even by despair, because of this.'

Aware of such a withdrawal of God's help, Gogol was now

entirely at the mercy of his own moral hypochondria, his fears of divine wrath and his peculiar *angoisse*, which he tried to relieve by praying and fasting. To him prayer was not mere prayer. As in the case of primitives, it was something of an incantation fraught with a magical power, provided it was accompanied by piety and repentance. Yet as these were generated in him mainly by fear, his own prayers, however frantic at times, left him spiritually cold. Thanks to his peculiar turn of mind, he saw in this very coldness only another sign that God no longer wanted even his prayers. 'Alas, it is not easy to pray,' Gogol complained on 12th February 1848 in a letter to a recent acquaintance of his, Father Matthew Konstantinovsky. 'How can I pray if God does not want me to! I see so much that is bad in me, such an abyss of selfishness and incapacity to sacrifice earthly things for the sake of the heavenly principle.... Only now I am appalled by my own conceit, wondering how it is that God has not yet struck me and wiped me off the face of the earth. ... I am burning with shame, and do not know how to hide my face—under the weight of the incredible number of vices and weaknesses, the presence of which in me I did not even suspect before.'

2

By thus magnifying his own vices and weaknesses, Gogol may have hoped to placate the God, Who, having turned away from him in this world, would judge him in the world to come. But since God remained silent, some more effective expedients had to be tried: the prayers of those people (especially if they were connected with the Church) who had a greater chance of being listened to by the Eternal Judge. 'Oh, do pray for me,' became from now on a frequent refrain in Gogol's letters. Like his artist-monk in *The Portrait*, he still hoped at times to 'earn the peace and inspiration he needed for his work by first purifying his spirit with toil, prayers and all the ascetic rigours he could think of,' but it was of no avail. His apathy was strengthened by his growing fear of human contacts—the kind of fear which verged at times on persecution mania. He also suffered from a feeling of continuous physical cold and of freezing, no matter what the temperature around was like. The few attractions that were still at his disposal left him indifferent. Even the beauty of his 'lovely far-away paradise' Italy seemed to have faded. 'He stood aloof and avoided society,' says Count Sollogub of his last years abroad. 'Gogol's reserve was almost eccentric. Not that he was afraid of people; he only regarded them as a nuisance. When someone wanted to see him, he would just disappear from his room. He could still be gay now and then; in the evenings he would read aloud from his works (only printed ones), or impersonate his former Nezhin teachers so comically that those present would split their sides with laughter. Yet his life was austere and sad. He read St John Chrysostom in the mornings, after which he would write and then tear up all he had written.' But such life could not go on indefinitely. Something had to be done in order to change it and to obtain at least one ray of hope. So Gogol thought in all seriousness of his pilgrimage to Palestine.

He had planned this journey as far back as 1842, but it was only now, at the height of his predicament, that he embarked upon it—as a last attempt to arrive at a solution In the worst case he expected to gain in Palestine some certainty as to whether God still wanted his services or not; whether or not his doom was irrevocable. If divine Grace was still available to him at all, then surely his heart would be kindled there, in the holiest places on earth, to a new creative and religious fervour. But all this was fraught with so many apprehensions that he never knew what exactly to expect and to hope for. And since his own prayers remained cold, he now preferred to rely on the prayers of those people whose intercession was more likely to reach God's ears. Only a few weeks before his departure, he wrote to Father Matthew (on 2nd December 1847): 'I am going to Jerusalem in order to pray at our Saviour's Tomb, to pray as much as possible. Do pray for me, good soul, so that I myself may be able to pray fervently and deeply. Do pray to God that on the very soil His divine Son had trodden my heart may reveal to me all I have to do. I wish that from the very first day of my worship I may carry the image of Christ in my heart wherever I go, and that I may all the time keep Him before my soul's eyes.' Yet the letter he addressed to him on 12th February 1848, almost on the eve of his departure, ended with the strange remark: 'It even seems to me that I have no religion. I confess Christ only because my reason and not my religion urges me to do so. . . . *I only wish to believe,* and in spite of this I now dare undertake a pilgrimage to our Saviour's Tomb. Oh, do pray for me.'

3

Gogol went to the Holy Land and stayed there for several weeks. But this time, too, he only had another disappointment. The pilgrimage, from which he had expected miracles, failed to ease his trouble mind. His habitual inner cold and chaos did not leave him even at our Saviour's Tomb. And when rain obliged him to stop for a couple of days at Nazareth, he felt—so he says—as if he were waiting at a dreary postal station somewhere in the Russian provinces. True to his restless nature, he began to wander about in Syria, where he was joined by the Russian consul at Beyrut, Basili—one of his former school-comrades at Nezhin. Basili did all he could to make his old friend's tour pleasant, but Gogol was far from appreciating his kindness. On the slightest pretext he grew excited, gesticulated like a hysterical woman, and shouted at Basili as though the latter were his servant. Apprehensive of his own prestige among the natives, Basili found it necessary to adopt the tone of a master. No sooner had Gogol felt a stronger will opposing his caprices than he became compliant, or even polite, and remained so till the end of the journey.

Gogol left Palestine without any signs of the inner regeneration he had longed for. Nor did he ever try to describe the holy places—an intention he had formerly spoken of to some of his friends. But since all the prayers he had poured out in Jerusalem had brought him no relief, his position was now worse than it had been before the pilgrimage. It was Belinsky who in his harsh letter had pointed out to him that 'one can pray anywhere, and only those people go to search for Christ in Jerusalem who either have never had Him in their hearts or who have lost Him. Those who suffer at other people's sufferings, and feel oppressed when others are oppressed, are the ones who carry Christ in their hearts, and there is no reason why they should go to Jerusalem.' True enough! Yet the honest atheist Belinsky had hardly understood the tortuous ways of Gogol's mind. Distressed by the archaic pattern of thought he was unable to cast off, Gogol could not but interpret the failure of his Palestinian journey in the sense that he was now doomed beyond recall. God, who had refused to relent even in Jerusalem, must surely have marked him as a candidate for hell and perdition. His fear of the Devil —the real Devil in whom he believed with the primitive faith of a child or a peasant—was therefore on the increase. So were his moral torments.

'I must tell you that never before have I been so little pleased with the state of my soul as I was in Jerusalem and since my stay in Jerusalem,' he wrote to Father Matthew from Odessa on 21st April 1848. 'There I only had an opportunity of seeing my own hardness and egoism—that is all.' Less than a month later he wrote in the same strain to Countess Nadya Sheremetyeva: 'It looks as if I was at our Saviour's Tomb only in order to feel *there*, in that very spot, the terrible coldness and egoism of my heart. That which I thought *near* is now *far away*. . . . It was with cold lips and with a hard soul that I continued to whisper the same prayers in the same old manner. . . . My friend, do pray for me.' He mentioned his 'heart's terrible hardness' also in his letter to Countess G. M. Sollogub—a letter in which he fully gave away the state of mind he was in after that deplorable journey. 'With horror I see in me nothing but sheer egoism, nothing but the truth that, despite my capacity for appreciating lofty feelings, I myself am utterly devoid of them and am even getting worse, while my character keeps deteriorating in such a way that each action on my part means an offence inflicted on someone. I am now more horrified about myself than ever before. I must tell you that often I have implored, secretly and without your knowing it, both you and Anna Mikhailovna[36] to pray for me with all your might. I do not know whether your hearts have sensed this. Yet each time when in my thoughts I imagined both of you praying for me, I felt easier, and hopes of God's mercy began to stir within me.'

Victimised by such moods and dispositions, Gogol no longer expected any miracles from his artistic efforts either. For however lofty his aim, the requisite creative impulse was absent. It is of no small interest that on 10th January 1848, that is before sailing to Jerusalem, he wrote a long letter to Zhukovsky in which he expressed his hope of being able to resume, after Palestine, his literary activities as a creator and not as a mere sermonizing *raisonneur* in the manner of *Selected Passages*. 'In truth, it is not my business to teach by means of sermons. Art itself is a lesson. My task is to speak in terms of *living* images, not by reasoning. I must show life as it is, and not reason about life.' An attitude sound enough in theory. But when, back from Palestine, he tried to put it into practice, he noticed with alarm that his creative process was slower than ever—a final proof of God's unwillingness to use him as His medium here on earth. His imagination made things worse by exaggerating his own moral unworthiness on the one hand, and by conjuring up pictures of the hell-fire and eternal torments on the other. Visions which thus kept haunting his mind were hardly conducive to good cheer. Another drawback was the fact that after his pilgrimage Gogol did not return to Italy, but settled (after a brief stay in the Ukraine) in Moscow.

N. V. Berg, who saw him there at the end of 1848, speaks of Gogol as a pale little man with small moustache, piercing dark eyes and a strangely mincing gait, 'as if one leg always wanted to jump forward, and that was why one step invariably came out longer than the other. There was something fettered in his entire figure, something tied and utterly repressed. No ease, no frankness, either in his eyes or gestures. The looks he cast around were not straight and direct, but sidelong, intermittent, and as though evasive.' The French author Melchior de Voguë described him (from an eye-witness's account) as a taciturn, shy and unprepossessing little man with short legs and a long nose which gave him a somewhat comic appearance. Count Sollogub saw Gogol for the last time in 1850, and this is what he says of the meeting: 'He came to say good-bye to me, and began to talk so disconnectedly, in such a vague and obscure manner, as to make me feel perturbed and alarmed. When I said something about the originality of Moscow, his face lit up, a spark of his former gaiety flashed into his eyes, and he told me, in his own peculiar manner, a most interesting and typical anecdote. But he suddenly grew sad again, and was entangled in such muddled talk that I saw at once he was past recovery.'

Of no less interest is Ivan Turgenev's impression of Gogol, whom he met in Moscow in October of the following year. 'His blonde hair, which from his temples was falling straight down in Cossack fashion, had still preserved the colour of youth, although it had grown noticeably thin. His bulging, smooth and white forehead expressed the same intelligence as ever. In his small brown eyes there still sparkled now and then gaiety—not a ridiculing disposition, but gaiety. Yet generally speaking, his eyes were tired. His long, pointed nose imparted to Gogol's face something sly and fox-like. An unpleasant impression was made also by his thick, soft lips protruding from under his clipped moustache. Their vague line suggested—such at least was my impression—certain dark features in his character; when he spoke, they opened in an unpleasant manner and showed a row of bad teeth. His tiny chin was hidden in his broad, black velvet cravat. In Gogol's movements there was something not exactly professorial but rather schoolmasterly—reminiscent of the teachers in a provincial grammar school.' But impressions apart, Gogol's difficulties, sufferings and inhibitions were further aggravated, during those last few months of his life, by his close association with Father Matthew Konstantinovsky.

4

Accounts of Father Matthew's personality vary. From what one can gather, this eloquent country priest from Rzhev, who had 'distinguished' himself by his persecution of the Russian dissenters, had an uncouth, one-track mind endowed with a spiritual lust for power. While still in Italy, Gogol was recommended to him in 1847 by Count A. P. Tolstoy and even sent him a copy of *Selected Passages*. But the reverend gentleman replied with an indignant letter in which he raged above all against Gogol's favourable attitude towards the theatre. The correspondence between them continued, as might be guessed, on soul-saving lines. On his return from Palestine to Russia, Gogol met the holy man for the first time in Moscow. If we are to believe Ivan Shcheglov, who investigated certain phases of Gogol's life, this encounter must have been strange indeed.

'What is your religion?' the priest asked, when Gogol was introduced to him.

'Orthodox.'

'Not Protestant?'

'By no means. I am not a Protestant, but Orthodox. I am Gogol.'

'To my mind you are simply a swine. What kind of an Orthodox Christian can you be, since you do not even beg of me God's Grace and my pastoral blessing!'

The reverend father was obviously far above such trivialities as human politeness. Narrow-minded enough to be all of a piece, he would not doubt for a moment that as a priest he was something of God's deputy here on earth. Gogol, considering the state of mind he was in, could hardly have wished for anything better. Who, if not a firm believer and a deputy of heaven in one, would show him the right path to God and save his frightened soul from perdition! Father Matthew saw what was the matter and, knowing his business, was soon able to play on the penitent author's fears with the skill of a virtuoso. When it came to the devil and hell-fire, he spoke with such relish of the torments awaiting condemned souls after death as to make his listener tremble like a frightened child and scream, 'Enough! Enough!' The effect of the hallucinations from which Gogol probably suffered was also far from soothing. 'Have mercy on me, O Lord! Bind Satan again through the power of Thy mysterious Cross,' he once scrawled on a piece of paper. It was during these painful weeks and months that he wrote a *Meditation on Divine Liturgy*—a kind of manual for the faithful attending Church service. The booklet, which was published posthumously, could have been written by any ecclesiastic, and was in fact reissued later by the Holy Synod. What makes this document interesting is its author's *will* to faith and piety, which comes out in the very tone of the *Meditation*. In the advice he gives to others one can feel his effort to force upon himself the religious warmth he speaks of. 'If the worshipper but follow each act [of the divine service] reverently and attentively, his soul will be uplifted: it will become possible for him to fulfil the Commandments of Christ; Christ's yoke will grow easy and His burden light . . . Great and incalculable may be the benefits of the Divine Liturgy if one but makes it a rule to carry its precepts out in life.'

Gogol had conflicts, though, with Father Matthew concerning literature. The fanatical priest knew little and cared less about *belles lettres*. He hated above all Pushkin, in whom he saw but a pagan and sinner. Apart from *Selected Passages* he had probably neither read nor even wished to read any of his victim's writings. Yet he tried to act as Gogol's arbiter in literary matters as well. Or rather he wanted Gogol to give up such a godless occupation as writing altogether, and concentrate his efforts only on the 'salvation' of his soul. But Gogol was still enough of an author to look for relief in literary pursuits, which alone were, perhaps, able to take him outside himself. On settling down in Moscow, he resumed his one-time study of Russian and Ukrainian folksongs, the beauty of which he could never resist. He learned Serbian in order to read the Yugoslav ballads collected by Vuk Karadjich, which had previously aroused the enthusiasm of Pushkin, Goethe and Jakob Grimm. He also continued to write, however slowly, the second volume of *Dead Souls*.

Whether he did or did not entirely finish it is a matter of conjecture. On 21st January 1850, for instance, Gogol wrote to Pletnyov: 'Practically all the chapters are now thought out or even jotted down . . . but only two or three of them have actually been written.' Yet during his stay near Kaluga in 1849, that is, some months earlier, Gogol had read nine chapters to Madame Rosset-Smirnova and a few to her half-brother Arnoldi.[37] Pletnyov says that in the summer of 1851 seven chapters were read by the author at a gathering. According to V. Chizhov's *The Last Years of Gogol's Life* (printed in *The European Messenger*, 1872) the second volume, like the first, consisted of eleven chapters which were ready for print. N. V. Berg actually mentions eleven chapters waiting in the same year to be taken to the publishers. Those people who had heard any portions of the manuscript were unanimous in their praise. Gogol, however, was not pleased either with the character or the slow progress of the second volume, which he was yet so anxious to bring to a satisfactory conclusion. 'What is this,' he complained in a letter to Zhukovsky, 'old age, or temporary paralysis of my strength? . . . My creative faculty is lazy. I am doing my best not to waste a minute; I hardly ever leave my writing-desk covered with sheets of paper, but the lines I write down shape themselves sluggishly. Or is it really possible that I am an old man at the age of forty-two?'

He *was* an old man; worse—a walking ghost. A slightly comic touch was added to Gogol's tragedy by the rumours circulating in Moscow at the time (1849–50) that he wanted, or was about, to marry the much younger Countess Anna Mikhailovna Vielgorskaya, whose consumptive brother Joseph had died in Rome—in 1839—literally in his arms. In a letter (probably sent to her in 1850) Gogol made an indirect confession of his attachment to her, or at least expressed his eagerness to find out what exactly their mutual relations were. The letter ended with 'Yours to the grave.' But even if Gogol's intentions were serious, he must have known that he was as little suitable for married life as were his undersexed heroes Shponka, Poprishchin and Podkolyosin. Moreover, Anna, whose family always welcomed Gogol as a guest and a friend, was of highly aristocratic stock, whereas he, with all his literary fame, stood on a much lower rung of the social ladder—not a small matter in those days. He may have dreamt of marriage simply as a man who was in need of a refuge or of an escape from a situation which he found increasingly desperate. But nothing came of his proposal, if it ever was made at all. So his sad and austere existence went on as before.

5

There was, however, one medium still likely to provide a temporary escape—the 'long, long road.' Gogol made ample use of it, this time in Russia. Now he was in Kaluga, then in Odessa, then in his native Ukraine. He hoped that travels of this kind and the observations he made would enable him to give a more reliable description of his country in the second and third volumes of *Dead Souls*. He even worked upon a geography of Russia—with all sorts of ethnographic, linguistic and other particulars. When during the last few weeks of his life travel, too, refused to help, he was confined to Moscow. His host, Count A. P. Tolstoy, made him feel comfortable enough, but Gogol would not think of comforts. Possessed by the *idée fixe* of damnation, he increased his self-inflicted torments, as though determined thereby to mitigate the vengeful Eternal Judge. Soon Father Matthew was on the spot again, and he saw to it that Gogol's mind should be properly attuned. He not only paid frequent visits to his victim, but for long periods stayed in the same house—periods which were doubtless filled with 'edifying' talks.

Things became worse after 26th January 1852, when Gogol's friend Madame Khomyakova (a sister of the poet N. M. Yazykov) suddenly died. Gogol was so depressed by her death that he developed symptoms of mental trouble. He could not get rid of the thought that he himself was now going to die. Unconsciously he probably wished for it, and (whatever his conscious fears of the 'beyond') regarded death as the only outlet from the impasse he was in. Gogol's certainty of his approaching death made the presence of Father Matthew more urgent than ever. Whether and how far he was responsible for

Gogol's burning of the second volume of *Dead Souls* is difficult to say. There is some evidence that on one occasion, when Gogol read him a chapter, Father Matthew became highly indignant at the way in which a priest was portrayed in it. It is known, moreover, that in January 1852 he and Father Matthew actually quarrelled. Yet after the priest's departure Gogol sent him (on 6th February) a letter in which he asked his forgiveness and once again expressed his submission to him. From that day on Gogol's physical and mental collapse doubled its pace. On the night of 11th February he prayed with exceptional fervour. Then he rose, called his boy-servant and, candle in hand, wandered through the rooms, crossing himself in each of them. Suddenly he took out of his portfolio a bundle of manuscripts, put them into the fireplace, and with his own candle set them on fire. Guessing what was the matter, the boy implored him in tears to spare the manuscripts.

'This is none of your business—you ought to pray,' replied Gogol. Then he waited until all the sheets had turned to ashes, crossed himself, kissed the boy, and went to his bedroom where he fell upon the divan and began to cry.

Among the manuscripts thus destroyed was the second part of *Dead Souls*. Did Gogol act in a fit of semi-madness, or was he entirely aware of what he was doing? And if he did it deliberately, what were the motives behind it? Was it an act of final self-abnegation on his part or only a half-hearted fulfilment of what Father Matthew had ordered him to do? Or did he burn the chapters, as in 1845, because he felt displeased with them and hoped to rewrite the whole of it at some future date? S. Aksakov says in a letter to Shevyryov (1852) that not long before his death Gogol had actually complained to Madame Aksakova that he would not let the second volume be printed, because everything in it was worthless and had to be rewritten. It is even possible that he had intended to destroy only those chapters of which Father Matthew disapproved, and by mistake burned much more. But all guesses are futile. So is the mystifying explanation Gogol gave to his host A. P. Tolstoy: 'Fancy how powerful the evil spirit is. I wanted to burn some papers which had to be destroyed, but I burned instead the chapters of *Dead Souls* I wished to leave to my friends after my death.'

Whatever the truth, one thing is beyond doubt: that Gogol's latent death-wish had become by this time even stronger than his fear of death. A few days after the burning of the manuscripts he refused to take any food at all. On 21st February O.S. (4th March) he died from exhaustion, and partly because of the doctors' stupid treatment. His last words were, 'Give me a ladder, a ladder!' Words reflecting, as it were, not only his archaic idea of heaven but also that symbolic notion of ascent which, for all its vagaries and aberrations, was yet present in him during the whole of his earthly life.

Conclusion

GOGOL DIED at the comparatively early age of forty-three. It is idle to speculate as to what he might have achieved had he lived longer and had he come to terms with himself and with the world. Even as it is, his work remains one of the great landmarks in Russian literature, while Gogol himself represents one of the most puzzling transition-figures between the romantic and the realistic periods in European literature as a whole. Unable to reconcile his archaic pattern of mind with a modern pattern of existence, Gogol was almost bound to use his art first as a romantic escape from, and then as an indictment of, that reality which he could not accept or endure. His accusations of life were intensified by his own moral pessimism, by his *angoisse*, as well as by those catastrophic moods which bring him strangely near to some present-day European authors. Another point he has in common with our age is his anxious enquiry into the meaning, and also into the moral and social responsibility, of art. An enquiry of this kind could not but mobilise all his ethical and religious propensities which, strong though they may have been, were distorted by his own inhibitions. The mixture of the archaic elements of a 'primitive' on the one hand, and of the restless quest of a modern *déraciné* on the other, only added to the difficulties which landed Gogol in all sorts of painful dilemmas, and eventually in a calamity he was unable to cope with, let alone avoid. This is why everything in him was either a puzzle or a misunderstanding.

The very fact that his champion, the critic Belinsky, proclaimed him the originator of Russian realism was something of a misunderstanding. For in doing this Belinsky failed to perceive behind Gogol's realistic method the mind and the attitude of a frustrated romantic. And this despite the fact that in *Selected Passages* Gogol himself referred to *Dead Souls*, for example, not as a true picture of Russia but as a 'caricature and a product of my own fancy.' It was above all on what he regarded as Gogol's realism, or critical realism, that Belinsky founded that 'natural school' of Russian fiction whose aim was to be true to 'nature,' i.e. to Russian life.

Fortunately for Russian literature, Belinsky's attitude bore an abundant harvest. It was under the auspices of the 'natural school' that in the second half of the 'forties such realists as Grigorovich, Dostoevsky, Turgenev, Goncharov, Herzen and the playwright Ostrovsky made their literary debuts. Anyway, the basis for a school of Russian realism was there, and—whether rightly or wrongly—Gogol was looked upon as one of its principal founders. 'Gogol's influence on Russian literature has been very great,' Belinsky wrote in 1847. 'It is not only that all the young talents have begun following the path trodden by him, but even some authors with established reputations have done the same and have abandoned their former manner. Hence the emergence of the school which our detractors hoped to humiliate by calling it "natural." '[38] N. G. Chernyshevsky, who in 1855-56 wrote nine essays on Gogol, proclaimed him father of an independent Russian literature in prose. The critic and poet Apollon Grigoryev—a remarkable figure in the 'fifties and early 'sixties—even said that 'all that is alive in contemporary *belles lettres* comes from Gogol, explains him and is explained by him.' Dostoevsky in particular started his career under the sign of Gogol's *Greatcoat* and *A Madman's Diary*. From the first he derived his humanitarian note of pity, and from the second his psychological (or pathological) trend. Much later he acknowledged—in his *Journal of an Author*—that the majority of Russian realists, including himself, had come 'from under Gogol's Greatcoat.' The big-city motifs and the hectic 'irrational' side of Petersburg, so conspicuous in Dostoevsky's novels, have also been anticipated, to some extent, by Gogol's Petersburg stories. Gogol's indictment and bitter laughter, on the other hand, with all the ethical censure implied, received a further impetus in the works of A. T. Pisemsky, and particularly in those of M. E. Saltykov-Shchedrin, as well as in the playwright A. V. Sukhovo-Kobylin. Chekhov himself inherited a great deal of Gogol's 'laughter through tears,' although in his last phase hidden tears prevailed. Nor should one omit the impact of such works as *The Revizor* and *Dead Souls* on the political and social consciousness of Russia.

Technically, too, Gogol's influence was far from negligible. Concentration on character at the expense of an involved plot became, after Gogol, an obvious device of Russian authors— with the possible exception of A. T. Pisemsky and N. S. Leskov, both of whom delighted in a richly articulated plot. The painstaking description of trifles, the *Kleinmalerei*, in I. A. Goncharov's novels, is only an extension of the method used by Gogol in *The Old-World Landowners*, *The Greatcoat*, and *Dead Souls*. Even the two principal characters, Oblomov and Stolz, in *Oblomov*, are largely a further elaboration of Tentetnikov and Kostanzhoglo in the unfinished second volume of *Dead Souls*. Gogol's agitated style, again, was adopted by Dostoevsky, from whom it passed to the modernist Andreï Bely, and from Bely to some Soviet authors as well. Lastly, as a pioneer of the *skaz*[39] Gogol found adroit followers in writers such as N. S. Leskov, A. Remizov, E. Zamyatin, and more recently M. Zoshchenko.

Another feature bequeathed by Gogol to Russian literature was his anti-Philistine trend; his fear of a dehumanised humanity, and also what might be called his metaphysical tedium which often seems to imply that something must be wrong with the very root of existence. The mood of Fyodor Sologub's famous novel, *Petty Demon* (*Melky bes*, 1910) can be regarded in this respect as a modernist counterpart of *Dead Souls*. And is it necessary to stress that Gogol's searching vexation of the spirit was both deepened and amplified in the works of Tolstoy and Dostoevsky? Nor did his endeavours to make literature an organic part of life fall on sterile ground. It was here indeed that Belinsky's 'natural school' came, once more, into its own. Belinsky taught that literature, in addition to being true to reality, should also become a dynamic vital force helping us to build up a better and worthier reality—life in the fullest sense of the word. But whereas Gogol hoped for a renovation of life by means of ethical and religious values (as he understood them), Belinsky laid stress on social justice, on the vindication of all the 'insulted and injured.' He actually anticipated several aspects of that socialist realism which, in our time, was systematized by Gorky, and has become the backbone of Soviet literature.

It is, of course, a far cry from the art of Gogol to the *littérature engagée* of Soviet Russia. Yet not a few ingredients of Soviet literature can be traced—via such critics as Chernyshevsky and Dobrolyubov—back to the Gogol-Belinsky era, or rather to Gogol as interpreted by Belinsky. So each successive period has taken something from Gogol—a fact which only proves the strange vitality of his art. His work, like the work of all true creators, still delights one generation after the other. And there is no doubt that it is strong enough to continue to do so, whatever the vagaries of literary tastes and fashions.

A Note on Gogol in Music and on the Screen

APART FROM Pushkin, there is hardly an author whose works are as popular with the Russian composers as those of Gogol. N. V. Lisenko (an Ukrainian) wrote in 1870 his opera *Christmas Eve*, in 1880 *The May Night*, and in 1890 *Taras Bulba*—all of them based on Gogol's stories.

One of Tchaikovsky's early operas (1874) was *The Blacksmith Vakula*. He took the motif from Gogol's *Christmas Eve* and changed its name some ten years later into *The Slippers* (*Cherevichki*). The same theme was used for an opera (in 1895) by Rimsky-Korsakov, one of whose youthful works, written in 1879, was another *May Night*.

Moussorgsky took the libretto for one of his best known operas, *The Sorochintsy Fair*, from the first tale in *Evenings on a Farm near Dikanka*. In 1868 he, moreover, set to music in colloquial prose (*opéra dialoguée*) the first act of Gogol's *Marriage*. The rest of it was completed more than fifty years later (in 1931) by the composer M. M. Ippolitov-Ivanov.

Gogol's story *The Nose* was turned, in 1929, into a satirical opera by D. D. Shostakovich. Another Soviet composer, K. N. Shvedov, remade *The Revizor* into an opera in 1935.

As for the screen adaptations of Gogol's works, *The Marriage* and scenes from *Dead Souls* were filmed as early as 1909; *Taras Bulba* (under the title *Andriy's Love*) in 1910; *A Horrid Vengeance* in 1913; *The Revizor* in 1914.

The Soviet film industry has so far made use of *The Sorochintsy Fair*, *Christmas Eve*, *Taras Bulba*, *The Greatcoat*, *The Quarrel of the Two Ivans*, *The Revizor* and *The Marriage*.

Recently a travesty of *The Revizor* was made by Hollywood under the title *The Inspector General*. But of this the less said the better. It is a pity that Gogol's name should have been attached to the film.

Notes and Comments

1 Although mediocre as writer and poet, Nikolai V. Stankevich (1813–40) was a remarkable personality. He studied at the Moscow University during the first half of the 'thirties (1831–4), when a new and highly idealistic spirit had set in. The students, keenly interested in the philosophy of Schelling and Hegel, formed various circles for the purpose of study. The most outstanding of these were the circle grouped around Stankevich and the one led by the gifted Alexander Herzen (1812–70). Whereas in the Stankevich circle the study of philosophy, art and literature was paramount, Herzen and his friends were more interested in social-political problems, as well as in the Utopian French socialism of the day.

2 Mikhail P. Pogodin (1800–75) was the son of a serf, but he obtained a sufficiently good education to become a well-known historian, journalist, and professor of the Moscow University. Between 1827 and 1830 he edited *The Moscow Messenger* (*Moskovsky Vestnik*) and later, from 1841 until 1856, *The Muscovite* (*Moskvityanin*). Like his friend, the critic, poet and historian of Russian literature, Professor Stepan P. Shevyryov (1806–64), he was a representative of that 'official nationalism' which emanated from the government. At the same time he had many points of contact with the Slavophils.

3 Sergei T. Aksakov (1791–1859), the author of *A Family Chronicle* and its continuation *Childhood of Bagrov-Grandson*, written partly under Gogol's stimulus, was a hospitable landowner of the old patriarchal type, who also had made a career in civil service. His sons, Constantine and Ivan, were well-known Slavophils.

4 He was particularly good in the role of Madame Prostakova in Fonvizin's comedy *The Minor*.

5 Faddei V. Bulgarin (1789–1859), a Pole by birth and a Russian journalist and author by profession, was a notorious opportunist and time-server of that period. From 1825 onwards he edited, together with N. I. Grech, *The Northern Bee*, in which he was one of the principal (and most unprincipled) critics. He also wrote novels and several historical narratives. In the latter he tried to emulate Sir Walter Scott.

6 Peter A. Pletnyov (1792–1862), from 1832 onwards professor of Russian literature at the University of St Petersburg, was a

minor poet but quite an influential critic belonging to the Pushkin circle. Owing to his aesthetic leanings, he was antagonistic to Belinsky. After Pushkin's death he became editor of *The Contemporary* (founded by Pushkin) and remained in that office from 1838 until 1846. From the outset he greatly admired Gogol's writings.

7 Count Vladimir A. Sollugub (1814–82) was above all a polished dilettante. In the 'thirties and 'forties he wrote stories (rather satirical of high society), vaudevilles, and scored considerable success with his *Tarantas* (1844)—a satirical literary *pastiche,* partly influenced by Gogol's *Dead Souls.*

8 Marlinsky was the *nom de plume* of Alexander A. Bestuzhev (1797–1837)—a Decembrist, first exiled to Siberia and then to the Caucasus, where he served in the army. During 1823–5 he published, together with the poet K. Ryleyev, the miscellany *The Polar Star,* in which he wrote a number of stories and also some able criticism directed against the pseudo-classical current. A great admirer of Byron and Hugo, he became the most popular romantic story-writer in the 'thirties. His rhetorical and flowery style resembled the 'furious' French school. His plots, too, were rather forced and artificial. On the other hand, he knew how to tell a story and also made use of Russian (and Caucasian) motifs. His narratives exercised a certain influence on Lermontov, but after the prose of Pushkin and Gogol, Marlinsky's popularity declined, until he became almost forgotten.

9 Ivan P. Kotlyarevsky (1760–1838) is regarded as the father of contemporary Ukrainian literature, whose starting point was his humorous and satirical parody of Virgil's *Eneid* (1798) adapted to Ukrainian conditions and local colour. He did for the Ukrainians what Lalli, with his *Eneide Travestita,* had done much earlier for the Italians, and Scarron, with his *Vergile Travesti,* for the French. There existed also a Russian parody by Osipov (published in 1791). Kotlyarevsky earned his wider popularity as author of the librettos for the two best known Ukrainian musical comedies: *Natalka Poltavka* and *The Muscovite Wizard* (*Moskal Charivnik*).

10 Such a study has been attempted in Soviet Russia by Professor I. D. Ermakov in his *Essay in the Analysis of Gogol's Creative Process,* 1923.

11 Mikhail N. Zagoskin (1789–1852) started his literary career as a playwright, but from 1827 onwards concentrated on novels. His *Yury Miloslavsky* (1829) was the first really successful Russian novel after the manner of Sir Walter Scott. As a writer he was more prolific than gifted. When Gogol first met him, Zagoskin was closely associated with the Moscow theatre.

12 Gogol himself was a great eater and knew how to appreciate good food—a feature which he projected, on a bigger scale, into Pyetukh (a character in the unfinished second volume of his *Dead Souls*).

13 Its present size and shape is taken not from *Mirgorod* as originally published but from the enlarged and much improved edition (twelve chapters instead of nine) of 1842.

14 The idea that Gogol was addicted to the vice of erotic self-abuse is taken seriously by quite a few of his biographers, especially by those who are concerned with the medical side of his ailments.

15 It also includes three literary fragments of minor importance: an allegorical poem called *Life*, *a Chapter from a Historical Novel* (first printed in 1831), and *The Prisoner*. The last two are fragments of a planned novel, *Hetman*, on the lines of Sir Walter Scott. He is believed to have written a considerable portion of this historical novel, most of which he then destroyed.

16 According to P. Karatygin's Memoirs, Petromikhali may have been suggested to Gogol by an actual usurer living in Petersburg— a picturesque Oriental (a Hindu) who, towards the end of the 'twenties, used to draw the attention of the passers-by, and perhaps also of Gogol, on the Nevsky.

17 In his book, *The Evolution of Russian Naturalism* (Leningrad, 1929), V. V. Vinogradov points out Janin's *L'âne mort et la femme guillotinée*, which appeared in a Russian translation in 1837, as having influenced *The Nevsky Prospect*. Somewhat far-fetched are his arguments concerning the influence of de Quincey's *Confessions of an English Opium Eater*.

18 When, in 1836, Pushkin began publishing his excellent quarterly *The Contemporary* (*Sovremennik*), Gogol printed in it, amongst other things, his *Petersburg Notes*, with an amusing comparison between Petersburg and Moscow. Before *The Nose* was offered to Pushkin, Gogol had sent its earlier version to the *Moscow Observer*, whose editor (Shevyryov) rejected it on the ground that it was 'dirty and vulgar.'

19 Mikhail S. Shchepkin (1788–1863) was, like Pogodin, the son of a serf. After an adventurous youth he was accepted in 1823 by the State Theatre in Moscow, where he played comic parts and soon became one of the best actors in the history of the Russian theatre. The main feature of his acting was absolute naturalness and sincerity.

20 *The Revizor* was published in the same year. Its second and final version appeared in 1842.

21   A very low-class family name in Russian. It is derived from the word *tryapka* (rag).

22   This fragment, dating from 1839–42, was first printed in 1842 in Pogodin's periodical, *The Muscovite*.

23   Pavel V. Annenkov (1812–87), a critic and author of reminiscences. He belonged to the Belinsky circle and was responsible for the first complete edition of Pushkin's works (1850–60). He also wrote a biography of Stankevich which he published together with Stankevich's valuable correspondence.

24   In a narrative, *Vakh Sidorov Chaikin*, by Vladimir Dahl, there is an almost identical motif. Dahl, whose *nom de plume* was Kazak Lugansky, published his story a year after *Dead Souls;* but it is quite possible that he had written it some time before, or he may have spoken about the theme to Pushkin who, in his turn, transmitted it to Gogol.

25   *The Russian Gil Blas* (1814) by Narezhny, another (several years later) by Simonovsky, and *Ivan Vyzhigin* (1829) by Bulgarin are among them. It was actually Gogol who put an end to cheap satirical didacticism of this kind.

26   The pet name for a bear in Russia is Mishka—a diminutive of Mikhail (Michael).

27   This idea of the devil as apotheosis of respectable yet vulgar mediocrity also comes out in Ivan Karamazov's nightmare, in which his interlocutor, the devil, is embodied in a battered but respectable and most conventional gentleman *qui frisait la cinquantaine*. (See Dostoevsky's *Brothers Karamazov*).

28   Taken from Pushkin's famous poem, *The Prophet*, the impact of which must have been felt also by Gogol.

29   There were a number of such converts among the Russian aristocrats of that period. This was partly due to the 'infiltration' of the Jesuits into Russian society, as well as into high-class education, especially in St Peterburg.

30   Wife of the famous Slavophil leader S. Khomyakov (1804–60), who was also a poet and an able lay-theologian.

31   In 1846 Ivan T. Panayev (1812–52) bought, together with the poet Nikolai A. Nekrasov (1821–78), *The Contemporary* from Pletnyov, and invited Belinsky to be its principal critic.

32   In his letter Gogol comforted Aksakov with the promise of 'spiritual'—in place of physical—sight.

33   Aksakov is here referring to Gogol's illness in 1845.

34   In this Gogol resembles Tolstoy, although the roots of Tolstoy's moralism were different from those of Gogol's.

35   For a number of years the very possession of Belinsky's letter —that *profession de foi* of Russian intelligentsia—was regarded in Tsarist Russia as a crime. It was mainly for reading Belinsky's letter to a gathering of the revolutionary Petrashevsky circle that young Dostoevsky was sentenced (in December 1849) to death and then sent to Siberia instead. The letter was printed for the first time in 1855 by Alexander Herzen in his Russian periodical *Polar Star*, published in London. In Russia it appeared in print in 1905, that is, fifty-eight years after it had been written.

36   Count Michael Vielgorsky's daughter.

37   Several years later (in January 1862), Arnoldi summed up the contents of those chapters in *Russian Messenger*.

38   The term 'natural school' was first used by Bulgarin (in *Northern Bee*, 22nd Nov. 1846) in derision of its tendency to depict ordinary human beings and aspects of life as they were in 'nature.' Belinsky, however, took up this label as the highest praise, and regarded the trend itself as Russia's peculiar contribution to literature.

39   Gogol's best example of the *skaz* genre is the story of Captain Kopeikin in the tenth chapter of *Dead Souls*.

Bibliography

A. SOME ENGLISH AND AMERICAN TRANSLATIONS OF GOGOL'S WORKS

The Works of N. Gogol, translated by Constance Garnett, 6 vols. Chatto & Windus, London.

Tales from Gogol, translated by Rosa Portnova. Sylvan Press, London.

Tales of Good and Evil, translated with an Introduction by David Magarshack. John Lehmann, London.

Diary of a Madman, Nevsky Prospect, translated by Beatrice Scott. Drawings by Donia Nachsen. Introductory Essay by Janko Lavrin. Lindsay Drummond, London.

The Diary of a Madman, translated by Prince Mirsky. Illustrated by A. Alexeieff. Cresset Press, London.

The Inspector: A Comedy. Calcutta 1890.

Revizor, translated for the Yale Dramatic Association by Max S. Mandell, New Haven, Conn. 1908.

The Government Inspector, translated and adapted by D. J. Campbell. Sylvan Press, London 1947.

Tchitchikoff's Journeys; or Dead Souls, translated by Isabel F. Hapgood. Crowell, New York 1886.

Dead Souls, with an Introduction by John Cournos. Everyman's Library, J. M. Dent, London.

Dead Souls, translated by George Reavey. Hamish Hamilton, London 1948.

B. SOME RECENT WORKS ON GOGOL (in Russian, English, French, etc.)

BELY, A., *Masterstvo Gogolya,* 1934.
BRAZOL, BORIS, *The Mighty Three* (the chapter on Gogol), 1934.
DANILOV, S. S., *Gogol i Teatr,* 1936.
ERMAKOV, I. D., *Ocherki po Analizu Tvorchestva Gogolya,* 1923.
GIPPIUS, V. V., *N. V. Gogol',* 1936.
KIREYEV, D. I., *N. V. Gogol',* 1929.
KOTLYAREVSKY, N. A., *Nikolai V. Gogol',* 1903.
LEGER, LOUIS, *Nicolas Gogol,* 1914.
MANDELSHTAM, I. E., *O kharaktere Gogolevskogo Stilya,* 1902.
MEREZHKOVSKY, D. S., *Gogol' i chort,* 1906.
               Lermontov ... Gogol', 1911.

MOCHULSKY, K. V., *Dukhovny Put' Gogolya*, 1934.

NABOKOV, V. V., *Nikolai Gogol*, 1944, 1947.

OVSYANIKO-KULIKOVSKY, D. N., *N. V. Gogol*, 1902.

PEREVERZEV, V. F., *Tvorchestvo Gogolya*, 1928.

ROZANOV, V., Two articles on Gogol at the end of his study of Dostoevsky's *Grand Inquisitor*.

SCHLOEZER, BORIS DE, *Gogol*, 1932.

SHENROK, V. J., *Materialy dlya Bibliografi Gogolya*, 4 vols, 1902–08.

VERESAYEV, V., *Kak Rabotal Gogol'*, 1934.

VINOGRADOV, V. V., *Evolyutsiya Russkoro Naturalizma (Gogol' i Dostoevsky)*, 1919.
                  Etyudy o Stile Gogolya, 1926.

WIJK, N. VAN, *Hoofdmomenten der Russiese Letterkunde* (the chap- on Gogol), 1919.